This book should be returned to any branch of the
Lancashire County Library on or before the date

Lancashire County Library
Bowran Street
Preston PR1 2UX

Lancashire
County Council

www.lancashire.gov.uk/libraries

D0716115

try it!

EAT MORE
VEGETABLES

by Carolyn Humphries

DK | Penguin Random House

DK INDIA

Project Editor Arani Sinha
Senior Art Editor Ivy Roy
Art Editor Jomin Johny
Deputy Managing Editor Bushra Ahmed
Managing Art Editor Navidita Thapa
Pre-Production Manager Sunil Sharma
Senior DTP Designer Pushpak Tyagi
DTP Designer Manish Upreti

DK UK

Project Editor Kathryn Meeker
Senior Art Editor Anne Fisher
Jacket Designer Amy Keast
Producer, Pre-Production Andy Hilliard
Producer Stephanie McConnell
Photography William Reavell
Cookery Editor Diana Vowles
Managing Editor Stephanie Farrow
Managing Art Editor Christine Keilty

First published in Great Britain in 2016 by
Dorling Kindersley Limited,
80 Strand, London WC2R 0RL

Copyright © 2016 Dorling Kindersley Limited
A Penguin Random House Company
2 4 6 8 10 9 7 5 3 1
001 – 290927– Jan/2016

A CIP catalogue record for this book
is available from the British Library.
ISBN 978-0-2412-4826-3

Printed and bound in China.

All images © Dorling Kindersley Limited
For further information see: www.dkimages.com

A WORLD OF IDEAS:
SEE ALL THERE IS TO KNOW

www.dk.com

Contents

Foreword

We all know that vegetables form a crucial part of our five-a-day – and whether you shop in a farmer's market, an independent green grocer, or a large supermarket, there is certainly no shortage of produce on offer.

With an abundance of sumptuous-looking veg available – from roots, tubers, and stems to flowers, vegetable fruits, and leaves – there is every reason for vegetarians and non-vegetarians alike to make vegetables a central part of their diet. Packed with mouth-watering vegetarian recipes, all carefully balanced to provide the required nutrients for a healthy diet, *Eat More Vegetables* celebrates this bounty of fresh produce.

Eating the seasons

I grew up in the country, where my father had a large vegetable garden. My brother and I always enjoyed helping him dig the potatoes, pull the lettuces, string the onions, and pick the beans. We were used to eating fresh, seasonal vegetables every day and what we didn't grow ourselves had been produced locally. I now have just a small garden and can only grow fresh herbs and the occasional tomato, bean, or courgette, but it doesn't stop me from continuing to enjoy fresh vegetables every day. In fact, today you can buy just about any vegetable from around the world thanks to – or rather, because of – international transport and refrigeration. It is worth remembering, though, that vegetables have proper seasons when they mature, still attached to their plants, taking nutrients from the soil and ripening in the sun. Many are plucked before they are ripe to be transported half way around the world, and never achieve their optimum flavour or texture. Large-scale global movement of produce also has a negative impact on the environment, with the fuel used drastically increasing the amount of carbon dioxide released into the atmosphere.

Brave new world

Thanks to new growing techniques, many vegetables that are native to tropical climates are grown in controlled conditions in cooler countries, giving us all a much wider choice. There is an argument that the polytunnels used for growing these vegetables spoil the look of the countryside and that fuel is sometimes needed to heat them to the required temperature – but we can't have it both ways. When progress provides work for local people and allows us to enjoy great, locally grown food, it should, I believe, be embraced.

When selecting fresh produce, remember to consider what season it is, decide whether the vegetables are likely to have been home-grown, and check their source before you buy. When shopping in farmer's markets you can be confident that the food has been produced in the local area, but nowadays supermarkets also tell you where their produce has come from so you can make informed decisions about the food you buy. Not only will this boost the local economy but it will also ensure that you are getting the tastiest and most nutritious vegetables available.

Making the right choice

When home-grown food isn't available, it's worth considering ethical trading. The Fairtrade Foundation is an independent body offering disadvantaged producers in the developing world a better deal for their produce. Many of the goods – not just vegetables – sold through the foundation may not be available to you at home and, therefore, make excellent additions to the shopping basket. By actively seeking them out, even if it means paying a little more, you will be making a much-needed difference to people who really need the help.

Fresh food at your fingertips

If you're not lucky enough to have a vegetable garden or allotment, try growing herbs on a windowsill, lettuces in a window box, or mushrooms from a kit in the airing cupboard instead. Visit local pick-your-own farms where freshness is guaranteed and produce can work out cheaper than in the shops. Another option is to go foraging. Mushrooms are the obvious choice but – and it cannot be stressed enough – only pick fungi if you know exactly what to look for. Other delicious wild plants include garlic, sorrel, and nettles. (Remember never to pull up roots or take too much, though, as wild plants must be allowed to propagate and continue to flourish in an area.)

Fresh isn't always best

It's worth highlighting that pulses – dried peas, beans, and lentils – are vital to many dishes for their protein and carbohydrate content. Also, for the record, frozen vegetables are just as nutritious as fresh and have an important role to play in a busy cook's life, so don't be afraid to keep plenty in the freezer for those meals in a hurry.

A word to the wise

While most cheeses are now suitable for vegetarians, a few of the ones called for in this book, such as Parmesan and Gorgonzola, contain animal rennet. In place of Parmesan, try using a hard Italian cheese called Vegetalia, or hard sheep's cheese. A blue cheese such as Dolcelatte is made with vegetable rennet and can be used instead of Gorgonzola. Also note that Worcestershire sauce contains anchovies, but vegetarian options, such as Henderson's Relish, are available as well.

More veg, please!

This book has been great fun to put together and I hope I have created some inspiring dishes to get your taste buds tingling. Use the ideas here as a starting point for your own repertoire and keep in mind that it is important to be bold when cooking vegetarian food. Experiment with new flavours, use lots of herbs and spices, and don't be afraid to mix and match – when leaves meet roots or tubers tangle with stems, the colours, textures, and tastes can be simply stunning!

Carolyn Humphries

Store-cupboard essentials

Discover how to select, store, use, and combine a wide range of fresh, seasonal vegetables – and find out about the many different herbs, spices, pulses, nuts, seeds, and oils that can help bring out the best in your recipes.

Introduction

In this chapter are the vegetables featured in the book, as well as information about seasonal availability, what to look for when selecting, and preparation guidelines.

It's important to store vegetables properly, too. Most should be kept in the chiller box at the bottom of the refrigerator and used within a week. The exceptions are whole, uncut onions, roots, tubers, and winter squashes, which should be stored in a cool, dark, frost-free place. On these pages you'll also find the herbs and pulses that can enhance the flavour of vegetables. There's information on perfect flavour pairings, too, so you can make the most of every ingredient in your store cupboard.

Variety is the key to a healthy, balanced diet. Aim to eat at least five portions of vegetables and fruit every day to get the essential vitamins, minerals, and fibre needed for good health and wellbeing. This includes frozen, dried, and canned (preferably in natural juice or water) fruit and vegetables, as well as pure juices. Cereals, grains, and potatoes are also important as they contain the complex carbohydrates needed for energy and warmth.

Pulses, nuts, seeds, soya beans and products such as tofu, and quinoa, a grain-like grass, make an ideal base for many vegetarian dishes and are a good source of protein (for body growth and repair), complex carbohydrates, and fibre. Eat a mixture of these to get the right balance of essential proteins, as they do not all contain complete, or whole, proteins. Nuts, seeds – especially flaxseed – and their oils, olive oil, leafy green vegetables, grains, and eggs are also an important source of the essential fatty acids omega 3 and 6 (for warmth, nerve function, and healthy nails, hair, and skin).

"Calcium is found in dried figs and apricots, green leafy vegetables such as spinach, kale, and spring greens, and in whole grains, nuts, and seeds."

"Eat foods rich in omega 3 and 6 – the essential fatty acids needed for warmth, nerve function, and healthy nails, hair, and skin."

Dairy products are a good source of calcium (for healthy teeth and bones) and protein. They contain saturated fats, though, so choose reduced-fat options if possible. (Coconut milk is also high in saturated fat, so look for a reduced-fat option unless you want a particularly rich and creamy result.)

Leafy green vegetables, pulses, and bread contain iron (for the production of red blood cells). These foods should be accompanied by produce rich in vitamin C, which aids iron absorption, so be sure to include plenty of red and yellow vegetables, fruit, and pure fruit juice in your diet. Avoid tea and coffee at mealtimes, however, as they impair iron absorption.

Fortified breakfast cereals and bread are a source of vitamin B12 (to help prevent anaemia and keep the brain and nervous system working well). This is the only vitamin not readily available in vegetables. Yeast extract is another good source of B12, which is good news for Marmite and Vegemite lovers.

Everything you need for a healthy, balanced diet is contained in this book, and keeping a well-stocked store cupboard will mean that you can create any of the recipes whenever the mood takes you.

Cabbages and leafy greens

Always choose firm cabbages and fresh-looking leafy greens.

« SAVOY CABBAGE
This crinkly-leafed variety has a sweet heart and tender leaves that are best shredded then lightly steamed, boiled, or stir-fried. The outer leaves are good stuffed. Best in winter.

WHITE CABBAGE ⌃
Popular as coleslaw or fermented as sauerkraut; also good steamed or stir-fried. Try with caraway or fennel seeds, and dried fruits. Best in winter and spring.

⌃ CAVOLO NERO
Also called Tuscan black cabbage, has dark, coarse, leaves that should be crisp and straight. Goes well with tomatoes, garlic, and olives. Available autumn and winter.

⌃ POINTED OR HISPI CABBAGE
Has an excellent, sweet flavour and even the outer leaves can be shredded and cooked. Particularly good stir-fried or lightly steamed. Best in spring.

BRUSSELS SPROUTS »
Steam, briefly boil, or shred in salads, soups, and stir-fries. Good with chestnuts and white beans. Small, firm ones are sweetest. Leafy Brussels tops can be cooked as greens. Best in winter.

SORREL ⌃
Use these lemon-flavoured spear-shaped leaves like spinach; best used fresh. Baby ones are delicious raw in salads. Available spring to autumn.

KALE »
The tight, curly, dark-green leaves have an intense flavour. Cut out any tough, fibrous stalks first. Use fresh, as it can turn bitter if stored too long. Best in autumn and winter.

GREEN CABBAGE ⌃
Numerous varieties are available and they are great all-rounders. Particularly good with nuts and celery or shredded in soups and stews. Available most of the year.

SWISS CHARD ⌃
Chop and cook in soups, stews, casseroles, and stir-fries, or separate leaves and stalks: wilt the leaves, steam the stalks. Available summer and autumn.

SPRING GREENS ⌃
Shred in soups, stews, stir-fries, and casseroles, or very finely shred and deep-fry for a few seconds as crispy "seaweed". Best in spring.

BABY SPINACH ⌃
Great wilted as a vegetable or added to stir-fries, soups, and stews; baby leaves are delicious in salads. Particularly good flavoured with nutmeg. Different varieties are grown throughout the year.

RED CABBAGE ⌃
Use finely shredded and braised, pickled, or marinated as a salad. It turns a lovely bright red when used with vinegar, lemon juice, or wine. Best in winter and spring.

PAK CHOI (BOK CHOY) »
Asian mustard greens with fleshy stalks and soft leaves. Steam baby ones whole; chop or shred larger ones and stir-fry, or use raw in salads. Best summer to winter.

13

Vegetable flowers

These beautiful vegetables make for sumptuous eating.

BROCCOLI (CALABRESE) »
Select firm, dark-green heads.
Avoid if yellowing, even slightly,
or if pliable. Separate into florets
and eat raw, steamed, or stir-fried.
Best in summer and autumn.

« WHITE CAULIFLOWER
Choose tight curds; avoid if bolting
(flowering). Steam whole; florets
are delicious as crudités, coated in
cheese sauce, in soups, stir-fries,
and braises. Good all year.

GLOBE ARTICHOKE »
Choose firm, tight, heavy heads
that have a short stalk. Avoid
those that are dry or opening.
Steam and eat the leaves, then
heart, or prepare the heart only.
Best in summer and autumn.

⌃ PURPLE SPROUTING BROCCOLI
Avoid thick, woody stalks or if tiny
yellow flowers are appearing on the
heads. Steam, boil briefly, or stir-fry.
Best in late winter and spring.

⌃ PURPLE CAULIFLOWER
Will keep its colour if cut in florets
and lightly steamed. Has a particularly
sweet, mild flavour. Use in place of
white cauliflower for any recipe.

Shoots and stems

Succulent vegetables that all grow above ground.

« WHITE ASPARAGUS
Grown without light to prevent it from turning green, white asparagus is highly prized for its delicate flavour and creamy texture. Often served cold. Best in spring and summer.

⌃ GREEN ASPARAGUS
The most common variety. Look out for sprue: the cheaper, slim "thinnings" of the crop. Steam, griddle, roast, or use in soup. Best in spring and early summer.

⌃ PURPLE ASPARAGUS
Often less fibrous than green varieties and slightly sweeter, so there is no need to pare even thicker stalks. Cook and serve as per green asparagus.

FENNEL ⌃
Has an aniseed flavour. Shred raw in salads, or quarter and braise or roast. Don't confuse with the wild fennel herb, which does not form a bulb. Best in summer and autumn.

GREEN CELERY ⌃
Has a pronounced flavour that is excellent with cheese, fruit, and nuts. Chop the outer leaves for flavouring soups and stews; use the hearts raw or braised. Best in autumn and winter.

WHITE CELERY »
More delicately flavoured than green, white celery can be either "self-blanching" or green celery that is earthed up while still growing. Use like green celery.

⌃ KOHLRABI
Tastes like a cross between white cabbage and a mild-flavoured turnip. Eat raw if very fresh, or stew, braise, or add to soups. Best in summer and autumn.

Salad leaves

There is a huge variety of tasty leaves available, some grown all year.

⌃ WATERCRESS
Sprigs of round, peppery-tasting leaves. Trim off thick feathery stalks before using in salads or as a garnish, or chop to flavour sauces, soups, and egg dishes. Available all year.

⌃ ROUND (BUTTERHEAD) LETTUCE
The large, outer leaves make perfect wraps instead of bread or are good cooked in soup; the heart leaves are excellent dressed (at the last minute) for a salad. Available all year.

« LAMB'S LETTUCE
Clusters of small, soft leaves with a sweet nutty flavour, also known as corn salad. Lovely in a mix of leaves for a salad, and makes a pretty garnish. Best in summer and autumn.

⌃ WHITE CHICORY
Also available red, has a bitter core that should be cut out before separating into leaves or chopping for salads. Fill whole spears with soft cheese, dips, or salsas. Good braised whole. Available autumn to spring.

« CHINESE LEAVES
Pale-green, creamy-yellow leaves with thick, fleshy white stalks, a crunchy texture, and a juicy, sweet flavour. Excellent steamed, used in stir-fries, or eaten raw. Best in autumn.

ROMAINE (COS) ⌃
Crisp, tall leaves with a sweet flavour. Torn in pieces, the classic leaf for Caesar salad; even the outer leaves can be used in salad. Best summer and autumn.

ICEBERG ⌃
Crisp and juicy, with a firm, tight head. Carefully peel off the outer leaves (discard if wilted) to use as a receptacle for cold or hot food; shred or tear up the inner leaves. Best in summer and autumn.

LITTLE GEM »
A small, tight lettuce with juicy round leaves. Use sautéed in halves or quarters, or enjoy raw. The whole leaves make good receptacles for pastes and salsas. Best from spring to autumn.

ROCKET ⌃
Has a pronounced peppery flavour. Usually served raw, but can be wilted on pizzas and in tarts; great for pesto. Keeps best if bought unwashed. Available all year.

⌃ **MIZUNA**
When young, the dark-green serrated leaves with thin, white stalks have a mild, slightly spicy, mustardy taste, similar to rocket. Cook large leaves like pak choi. Best in winter.

« **PEA SHOOTS**
The tender young tops and tendrils of pea plants, these have a sweet, pea flavour. Perfect for salads and sandwiches (handle carefully as they are delicate). Available late spring and summer.

The onion family

When cooked, alliums take on an irresistible, creamy sweetness.

⌃ ROUND SHALLOTS

With sweet, mild, purple-tinged flesh, use finely chopped in any dish needing a delicate onion flavour. Good for pickling and in dressings, too. Best from autumn to spring.

BROWN ONIONS ⌃

Excellent all-rounders with gold to brown skins and a fairly strong flavour. Baby ones are used for pickling or cooking whole. Best in late summer and autumn.

« BANANA SHALLOTS

These torpedo-shaped shallots are highly prized by cooks for their sweet, delicate flavour. Use like round shallots. Best from autumn to spring.

⌃ RED ONION

With a sweet and mild flavour, use thinly sliced in salads; also great roasted, but a good all-rounder. Best in late summer and autumn.

WHITE ONION »

With white flesh and a sweet, mild flavour, this doesn't have to be fried-off before adding to a dish. Popular eaten raw in cheese sandwiches. Best in late summer.

« BABY LEEKS
Tiny, sweet leeks that are best steamed, griddled, or roasted whole for a starter or side dish. Sometimes called "poor man's asparagus". Best in autumn.

LEEKS ⌃
Have white bases, green tops, and a mild onion flavour. Use raw sliced or chopped in salads, or sauté, roast, steam, or boil. Keep wrapped in the fridge chiller box. Best in autumn and winter.

DRY GARLIC ⌃
The mature crop is hung in bunches to dry and is then stored for use all year. The pungent cloves are used individually. Whole heads can be roasted, then mashed.

« SPRING ONIONS
Use these bunched thin onions with green stalks in salads, salsas, stir-fries, and many other dishes. Avoid if browning and wilted. Best in spring and summer.

« FRESH GARLIC
Fresh and green garlic are interchangeable. Fresh garlic is the new season's mature crop, while young, green garlic (which looks like spring onions) is available in spring.

19

Store-cupboard essentials
Roots and tubers

These staples of the vegetable world are full of nutrients and flavour.

TURNIPS »
Baby turnips are mild; larger ones have a mustard-like kick. Peel thinly and grate raw, or dice, boil, or steam. Baby ones (use whole) are available in summer; larger ones all year.

MARIS BARD POTATOES »
Small, earthy-tasting new potatoes like these are harvested in summer. They have thin skins that should scrape or scrub off easily. Steam or boil.

« PINK FIR POTATOES
Small, waxy, round, and fingerling varieties like these are good steamed or boiled, whole or halved, and served warm or cold with salad. Best in summer and autumn.

« DESIREE POTATOES
This Dutch variety is a good all-rounder (much like Maris Piper). With fairly firm flesh, they are neither too floury nor too waxy and good for general potato cooking. Great for chips.

SWEET POTATOES »
Not actually related to the potato, these tubers have sweet creamy-yellow or orange flesh. Can be cooked just like potatoes, with or without skins. Available all year.

KING EDWARD POTATOES ⩓
This floury variety has a dry texture, which becomes "fluffy" when cooked. Good for roasting, mashing, baking, and for chips.

DAIKON ⩔
Also known as mooli or white radish. Originally from Japan, it has a strong taste similar to turnip or a hot radish and can be used in the same way as either. Best in summer and autumn.

⩓ YUKON GOLD POTATOES
This waxy variety has a firm, yellow flesh with a buttery flavour. Best boiled, steamed, baked, or for potato wedges.

BEETROOTS »
These round roots have firm skin and red, golden, or pink and white-striped flesh. They have a rich, sweet, earthy flavour. Serve raw or cooked, grated, sliced, or diced. Best from summer to winter.

BUNCHED CARROTS »
These sweet, fragrant summer carrots can be scrubbed and grated raw, or lightly cooked. The greens should be fresh and bright, but remove before storing or the carrots will go limp.

« PARSNIPS
The sweetness and creaminess of parsnips are most intense in winter. Look out for baby ones to cook whole. Steam, boil, roast, or grate raw.

« JERUSALEM ARTICHOKES
These tubers have a sweet, smoky flavour. Scrub or peel before use and choose ones with fewest knobs. Delicious in soup; also roast, steam, boil, or purée. Best from autumn to spring.

« RADISHES
Small, red, pink, or purple spheres, with a hot, peppery taste, or milder, longer-bodied breakfast varieties. Use raw or cook in place of turnips. Best in spring and autumn.

⌃ MAINCROP CARROTS
These are mature carrots that, once harvested, are stored for use during winter. Purple and yellow or white varieties are also available. Don't buy if over-chilled and damp.

SWEDE »
A large vegetable with thick outer skin and sweet, orangey-gold flesh. Delicious roasted or mashed, and in soups, stews, and casseroles. Best during winter.

⌃ CELERIAC
Creamy textured with a strong, sweet, celery-like aroma and flavour. Peel thickly then grate raw, or boil, steam, mash, or roast. Great for low-carb chips. Best in autumn and winter.

CHANTENAY CARROTS »
Originating in France, these very sweet cone-shaped carrots can be just trimmed and cooked whole; larger ones can be quartered lengthways. Best in summer.

Squashes and cucumbers

Winter squashes need cooking, while summer ones can be eaten raw.

BUTTERNUT SQUASH »
The skin should be hard; if soft, it is unripe and won't be sweet. Steam, boil, roast, purée, or halve and stuff. Keeps well in a cool, dark place. Best in autumn and early winter.

⌃ GREEN COURGETTES
Use raw, steamed, boiled, griddled, fried, or stuffed and baked. Small ones have the best texture. Stuff, batter, and fry the flowers. Best from May to October.

YELLOW COURGETTES »
Similar to green courgettes, but with bright-yellow skins and a more pronounced, slightly creamier flavour. Use in place of, or in combination with, green courgettes.

PUMPKIN »
From little ball to boulder-sized, with bright-orange flesh. Cook and purée for soups or pumpkin pie; also good roasted or steamed. Use instead of butternut or other winter squash. Best in autumn.

COMMON INDOOR CUCUMBER ⌄
Long, smooth, and green with mild-tasting flesh. Avoid if pliable. Eat raw, stir-fried, or try steamed with cheese sauce. Best in summer and autumn.

⌃ OUTDOOR RIDGE CUCUMBERS
Have knobbly, marked skins (but avoid if scabby). The flesh is crisp, firm, and slightly acidic. Some are very small and used for pickling. Available in summer and autumn.

Beans and pods

Some are eaten pods and all, others are shelled before use.

BROAD BEANS ⌃
The beans inside the pods should feel no bigger than a thumbnail; if larger, the skins can be tough, so remove them after cooking. Best from early summer through autumn.

GARDEN PEAS »
Choose bright-green, full pods, but where you can feel the individual peas. If too full or the pods are yellowing or shrivelling, the peas will be tough and the sugar will have begun to turn to starch. Eat fresh as their sweetness lessens on keeping. Best in summer and autumn.

⌃ GREEN BEANS
Numerous varieties are available, from string-width to the size of a pencil, with varying intensities of flavour. Top and tail then steam or boil whole, or cut in lengths. Good briefly blanched for salad. Best in summer and autumn.

⌃ MANGETOUT
French for "eat all", which describes how they're eaten. Simply snap off the stalk end and steam, boil briefly, or stir-fry. Choose bright-green pods that are crisp and squeaky. Best in summer and autumn.

SUGARSNAP PEAS ⌃
Rounded pods that contain small, very sweet peas. Eat whole steamed, stir-fried, or very lightly boiled, or chop into pieces and add to salads. Sweetest if eaten fresh. Best in summer and autumn.

Vegetable fruits

Although classed as fruits, the following are all eaten as vegetables.

FUERTE AVOCADOS »
Larger than Hass with smooth, shiny green skins. They have a mild flavour and pale-yellow flesh that slices well. Use like Hass. Ideal for salads and salsas. Best from winter to early summer.

⌃ HASS AVOCADOS
The rough skin turns black when ripe. Halve and fill cavity, purée, mash, slice, or dice. Can be baked. A good choice for dips and spreads. Best from spring to autumn.

« AUBERGINES
Also known as eggplants because of their ovoid shape. Baby ones, stripy pink and white, white, or tiny pea varieties are also available. All have a slightly smoky, sweet flavour. Roast, griddle, fry, or purée. Best in summer and autumn.

BABY CORN »
A specialist vegetable, deliberately grown to be harvested before the kernels develop. Eat whole or chopped in pieces, raw, steamed, boiled, or in stir-fries. Best in late summer and early autumn.

SWEETCORN »
Cobs (ears) are harvested when the kernels are just ripening. Pick pale-looking corn and eat fresh; golden, riper corn is not as sweet. Best in late summer and early autumn.

⌃ RED SWEET PEPPER
A member of the *Capsicum* genus, the plant also produces green, yellow, and orange fruits according to ripeness (and even purple or white ones). Use in any recipe calling for sweet peppers. Best in summer and autumn.

⌃ BIRD'S-EYE CHILLIES
Also known as Thai chillies, these are thin and tapering (approx. 3–7.5cm/1¼–3in long). As a rule, long, thin chillies such as these are hotter than long, fat ones, such as jalapeños. Often used in Thai and Indian cooking. Hot.

⌃ JALAPEÑO CHILLIES
Shiny, green or red, large, and cone-shaped. Also available pickled. Can be stuffed and are particularly good in Mexican cooking. Moderately hot.

SCOTCH BONNETS »
Said to resemble a Scottish tam-o'-shanter hat, these crinkly, rounded chillies are available in a variety of colours. They are popular in Caribbean cooking and are similar to habanero chillies. Extremely hot.

BEEF TOMATOES ⌄
Large, fat tomatoes that can weigh up to 450g (1lb) each. Excellent stuffed and baked, or sliced for salads and sandwiches. Best in summer and autumn.

ROMANO PEPPERS »
Spear shaped and longer and flatter than sweet peppers, these are very sweet. Usually available as red or yellow fruits, they are good stuffed whole, or split first then grill or roast. Best in summer and autumn.

« BABY PLUM TOMATOES
A tiny, plum-shaped variety with a very sweet flavour. Particularly good halved or whole tossed in pasta, rice, or other grain-based dishes (add near the end of cooking). Best in summer and autumn.

« PLUM TOMATOES
Oval-shaped, these are excellent for cooking as they have more pulp and less juice than other varieties. Very good for tomato sauce and widely used for perserving. Best in summer and autumn.

⌃ STANDARD TOMATOES
The classic round tomato. An excellent all-rounder for grilling, frying, slicing, or for salads. Buy on the vine for the most flavour. Best in summer and autumn.

⌃ CHERRY TOMATOES
Baby versions of standard tomatoes. Best bought on the vine to eat whole or halved in salads, or thrown into dishes towards the end of cooking so they hold their shape. Best in summer and autumn.

Mushrooms

Only forage for wild mushrooms if you know exactly what to look for.

⌃ BUTTON MUSHROOMS

These cultivated white mushrooms are picked at various stages of growth (from tiny button ones, through closed-cup, to large open-cup or flat mushrooms). The flavour develops as they grow. Eat raw or cooked, whole, sliced, or chopped. Also available dried.

⌃ FIELD MUSHROOMS

These wild white mushrooms have gills varying from pink to almost black. They are found in meadows where horses, sheep, or cows graze. Very good flavour. Large, flat ones may be peeled before use. Grow wild in autumn.

« MOREL MUSHROOM

Highly prized and sought after, the morel is found in woodlands (particularly ash and elm). It has a honeycomb hood and a rich flavour. Often sold dried. Grows wild in spring and early summer.

« NAMEKO MUSHROOMS

A cultivated mushroom very popular in Japan. Has an earthy flavour and a silky, almost gelatinous texture when cooked in stir-fries and soups. Trim off the base and separate the mushrooms before use.

« CEP MUSHROOM

Found in woodland clearings, particularly beech, this mushroom is also known as porcini in Italian cuisine. It is meaty and delicious with smooth, creamy flesh. Available dried. Grows wild in autumn and early winter.

⚡ OYSTER MUSHROOMS
Delicately flavoured, pale grey (or sometimes in pastel shades of brown, yellow, or pink), silky mushrooms favoured in Asian cookery. Cut up or cook whole. Often cultivated, but grow wild in autumn and early winter.

ENOKI MUSHROOMS »
Originally from Asia, these cultivated pale clumps have a crisp texture and a mild mushroom flavour. Trim and separate the mushrooms into smaller groupings before use in stir-fries, salads, wraps, and sandwiches.

⚡ PORTOBELLO MUSHROOMS
These cultivated brown mushrooms have a meaty texture and a good flavour. As with white cultivated mushrooms, these are picked at various stages of growth, from crimini (button), through chestnut (cup), to portobello (large and flat). Use like field or white mushrooms.

⚡ CHANTERELLE MUSHROOMS
Have a yellow or orange trumpet shape, a frilly top, and gills running down the stem. Found in many woodlands, but also cultivated and available dried. Have a slight smell of apricots and a delicious flavour. Grow wild from summer to winter.

⚡ SHIITAKE MUSHROOMS
Cultivated mushrooms originally from Asia with a brown cap and white gills. Have an excellent, meaty flavour that is particularly good in Chinese- and Japanese-style dishes. The stalks are often tough so remove and use for stock. Also available dried.

Pulses

These are all rich in proteins, carbohydrates, and fibre.

ADUKI BEANS ⌃
Richly coloured with a good, sweet, nutty flavour, they are excellent all-rounders that hold their shape well. Great in casseroles, soups, and stews. Also good for burgers.

BORLOTTI BEANS ⌃
Big, brown, rich, meaty, and with a lovely creamy texture, these beans are excellent in pasta dishes, stews, soups, and bakes as they hold their shape, even when cooked for a long time.

« BUTTER BEANS
Large, soft, and floury with a slightly dry texture when cooked, these beans have a distinctive, rich flavour. They are great for soups, stews, dips, and pâtés.

CANNELLINI BEANS »
A member of the haricot family, these classic Tuscan white beans can be mashed to a smooth paste. They have a creamy, slightly nutty flavour.

BROWN LENTILS ⌃
There are several varieties of brown (and green) lentils, which are interchangeable. All have a nutty flavour and a soft, almost meaty texture, making them a great substitute for minced meat in many dishes.

PUY LENTILS ⌃

These small, green lentils from France are often considered an upmarket ingredient. Particularly good braised with vegetables. They have an earthy, rich flavour and hold their shape even after cooking so are also good in salads.

FLAGEOLET BEANS ⌃

These pretty green beans have an excellent, creamy texture and a mild, sweet flavour. They are particularly good in salads, but also take on flavours such as garlic and herbs extremely well.

RED KIDNEY BEANS ⌃

Robust, floury-textured beans with a sweet, full-bodied flavour. They taste particularly good with chilli peppers and strong spices.

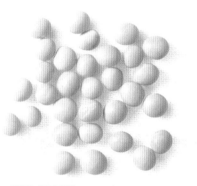

SOYA BEANS ⌃

Highly nutritious, these silky-textured beans have a mild flavour, which makes them a good base for complex flavour combinations. Also used for making other soya products such as tofu.

CHICKPEAS ⌃

These coarse pulses have a distinctive, nutty flavour and a buttery texture. They hold their shape even after long cooking. Also use puréed for dips (particularly hummus) and sauces.

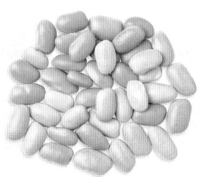

« HARICOT BEANS

Popular small, white beans, famous for their role in cassoulet, and as baked beans in tomato sauce. Excellent all-rounders for soups, stews, and casseroles with a mild flavour and a soft, creamy, yet slightly floury texture.

YELLOW SPLIT LENTILS »

Unlike yellow split peas, lentils hold their shape when cooked (although, for chana dhal you can substitute split peas; the result is just more pulpy). They have a distinctive, nutty flavour.

RED LENTILS ⌃

Small, split lentils that cook quickly to a pulp. They are ideal for soups and sauces as they thicken the liquid naturally. Also essential for spicy dhals.

Herbs

Imparting fragrance and flavour, herbs will lift any dish to a new level.

⌄ MINT
Many varieties are available, but spearmint and garden mint are the most common for flavouring. Dried mint is often used in Middle Eastern and Indian cookery. Good with potatoes, peas, lettuce, cucumber, yogurt, bulgur, rice, and lentils.

⌄ DILL
A delicate and feathery herb with a mild aniseed flavour. Seeds are also used for flavouring. Good with beetroot and other roots, broad beans, courgettes, potatoes, spinach, rice, and eggs.

ROSEMARY ⌄
Has a flowery fragrance. Use sprigs whole then remove after cooking, or chop leaves and add. Good with peppers, aubergines, lentils, mushrooms, onions, parsnips, and tomatoes.

« OREGANO
Interchangeable with marjoram with a strong, sweet flavour. Dried is popular in Greek and Italian cuisine. Add fresh at the end of cooking. Good with most vegetables, rice, pasta, and pulses.

« CORIANDER
Sweet and pungent, loved or hated, with thin, frilly-edged leaves similar to flat-leaf parsley. Its seeds are dried and used as a spice. A must for curries and spicy dishes; good with avocados, cucumbers, root vegetables, and sweetcorn.

« MARJORAM
Interchangeable with oregano and similar in flavour but slightly spicier. Dried is often used in its own right in Greek and Italian cuisine. Add fresh at the end of cooking. Use with most vegetables, rice, pasta, and pulses.

« CHIVES
These grass-like stalks have an aroma and flavour between onions and leeks. Snip with scissors. Add stalks and flowers as a garnish before serving. Use with avocados, courgettes, potatoes, root vegetables, cream cheese, and eggs.

« DRIED BAY LEAVES

Have a sweet fragrance reminiscent of cloves and basil. The leaves (both dried and fresh) are used to impart their flavour in a dish, but are not eaten. Essential for béchamel sauce and good with tomatoes, pulses, chestnuts, and rice.

⌃ SAGE

Pale, felt-like, greenish-grey leaves with a stringent, spicy, sweet yet bitter taste. Use sparingly in cooking. Lovely fried for a garnish. Good with pulses, cheeses, onions, and tomatoes.

« FLAT-LEAF PARSLEY

Italian flat-leaf parsley is favoured by cooks. Use on its own or with other herbs. Perfect chopped, in sprigs, or deep-fried as a garnish. Use with most vegetables, eggs, rice, lentils, and bulgur.

« COMMON PARSLEY

Readily available, common parsley is good for basic flavouring and as a garnish. Use a sprig tied with bay leaf and thyme for a simple bouquet garni.

« CHERVIL

Chervil's feathery leaves have an unusual sweet, spicy aroma with a hint of caraway. Don't cook. Particularly good as a garnish with asparagus, peas, beans, beetroot, carrots, tomatoes, cheese, and eggs.

⌃ BASIL

Has a warm, heady, slightly peppery flavour. Look out for Greek and Thai basil (*horapa*) too. Add at the end of cooking. A must for green pesto and pistou; also good with tomatoes, aubergines, beans, courgettes, eggs, and mozzarella cheese.

GARDEN THYME »

There are many varieties of thyme, but garden thyme is the most common. Has a sweet, spicy, soothing scent. The tiny leaves are stripped off the stem and added whole or chopped during cooking. Good with most vegetables.

TARRAGON »

Long, soft, thin leaves with a distinctive spicy–sweet fragrance and a pungent aniseed flavour. Use sparingly. Good with artichokes, asparagus, courgettes, mushrooms, potatoes, and tomatoes.

Techniques

Slice, dice, deseed, peel, pummel, and knead your way to culinary perfection with these essential step-by-step techniques. Find out how to prepare and cook your favourite vegetables, herbs, and spices.

Techniques
Dicing onions
Slice thickly for large dice and thinly for fine dice.

1 Using a sharp chef's knife, hold the onion firmly in one hand, then cut it in half lengthways. Peel off the skin, but leave the root intact so that the layers are held together.

2 Lay one half on a chopping board, cut-side down. Make a few slices into the onion horizontally, making sure that you cut up to, but not through, the root.

3 Hold the onion firmly, then, with the tip of the knife, slice down vertically, cutting close to the root. Repeat, slicing at regular intervals.

4 Cut across the slices for even dice. Use the root to hold the onion steady; discard this part when the rest of the onion has been diced.

Washing and slicing leeks

Leeks are related to onions, but have a much milder flavour.

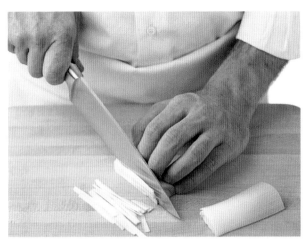

1 Trim off the root and some of the dark leaf top. Cut in half lengthways. Spread the layers apart and rinse well to remove any soil, then pat dry.

2 Lay the halved leek, flat-side down, on the chopping board and slice it into thick or thin strips, according to the recipe.

Peeling and chopping or crushing garlic

Garlic needs to be chopped or crushed to release all of its flavour.

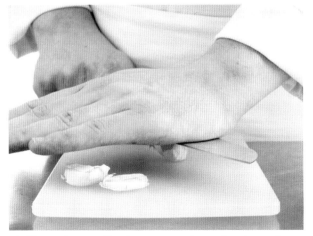

1 Place the garlic clove on a chopping board. Push down with the flat side of a large knife; this makes it easier to peel. Cut off the ends.

2 Slice lengthways, then cut across into tiny chunks. Collect them into a pile and finely chop again or crush with the flat of the knife.

Peeling and deseeding tomatoes

Choose firm tomatoes; vine-ripened ones have the best flavour.

1 Hold the tomato steady and use a sharp knife to score an "X" through the skin at the base. Immerse completely in boiling water for about 20 seconds, or until the skin splits.

2 Using a slotted spoon, carefully remove the tomato from the boiling water and immediately plunge it into a bowl of iced water to cool it.

3 When the tomato is cool enough to handle, use a paring knife to peel off the skin, starting at the base where the "X" was made.

4 Slice the tomato in half, then gently squeeze the seeds out and discard. Place the seedless tomato on a board, hold firmly, and slice into strips.

Peeling raw beetroot and cutting into batonettes

Raw beetroot can also be very thinly sliced or grated.

1 Hold the beetroot firmly in one hand and peel the skin thinly, using a vegetable peeler or small paring knife. If you wish, wear latex gloves to keep your hands from getting stained.

2 Place the beetroot on a clean chopping board and hold it steady. Use a chef's knife to trim the sides, doing this as evenly as possible to form a square shape.

3 Hold the trimmed block gently but firmly. Cut into equal slices – 3mm (⅛in) thick for juliennes and 5mm (¼in) thick for batonettes.

4 Stack the slices a few at a time to prevent them from sliding. Cut each batch into square-edged strips as thick as the slices.

Making courgette batonettes
Young courgettes with glossy skins will not need peeling.

1 Place the courgette on a board and cut off both ends. Cut it in half lengthways, then hold it on its side and cut into slices 5mm (¼in) thick.

2 Put each slice on the board and cut across with a sharp chef's knife to make equal-sized batonettes, about 5mm (¼in) wide.

Making carrot batonettes
For the best flavour, scrape young carrots; older ones need peeling.

1 Set the mandolin blade to a thickness of 5mm (¼in) and hold the mandolin steady. Slide the carrot up and down to make uniform slices.

2 Stack the carrot slices and cut in half crossways. Trim off the rounded sides, then cut the slices lengthways into equal strips.

Preparing asparagus
Look for fresh, sprightly spears with tightly closed tips.

1 Lay the spears on a board with the ends in line. Cut off about 2.5–4cm (1–1¾in) of woody stem. If very fresh, the stems can be snapped off.

2 To ensure tender spears, hold the tip very carefully, then use a vegetable peeler to peel off a thin layer of skin from all sides of the stalk.

Preparing sweetcorn
Sweetcorn tastes best when used fresh rather than tinned or frozen.

1 Remove the husks and all the silk thread from the corn. Rinse the husked corn under cold running water.

2 Place the blunt end on a chopping board. Using a sharp chef's knife, slice straight down the cob. Rotate the cob and repeat.

Preparing whole artichokes

Look for artichokes with tightly closed leaves and firm stalks.

1 Put the artichoke on a chopping board and hold firmly by the stalk. Then, with a pair of strong kitchen scissors, snip off the tough tips of the outer leaves.

2 Next, using a sharp chef's knife, cut through the stalk at the base of the artichoke head. Alternatively, if it is very fresh, twist off the stalk and the connective strings will come away, too.

3 Pull out any tough, darker-green leaves and discard. Cut through the pointed tip. The artichoke is now ready to cook.

Eating whole artichokes

Steam in a vegetable steamer for 30 minutes. Dip the fleshy leaves in melted **butter** or **French dressing** and draw between your teeth to scrape off the flesh. When the outer leaves are eaten, pull away the cone of pale inner leaves, scoop out the choke underneath, and eat the succulent heart.

To **roast**, scoop out the cone and choke. Stuff with **breadcrumbs**, **Parmesan cheese**, and **olive oil**, and roast.

Preparing artichoke hearts

Make sure you remove the hairy choke as it is inedible.

1 Place the whole artichoke on a chopping board. Carefully cut or pull away all of the leaves from the artichoke first, then cut the stalk from the base and discard.

2 Hold the artichoke firmly on the board and, using a sharp knife, cut off the soft middle cone of leaves, which can be found just above the hairy choke.

3 Trim away the bottom leaves with a paring knife. Scoop out the hairy choke if you plan to cut the heart into pieces for cooking.

4 Using a spoon, scoop out the choke fibres. Rub the exposed flesh with lemon juice to stop it browning.

Preparing avocados

Once ripe enough to eat, avocados are easy to peel and stone.

1 Hold the avocado firmly in one hand then, with a chef's knife, slice straight into the flesh, making sure that you cut all the way around the stone.

2 Once the avocado has been cut all the way around, gently twist the two halves in opposite directions and carefully pull them apart to separate them.

3 Strike the cutting edge of your knife into the stone and lift the knife (wiggling it if need be) to remove the stone from the avocado.

4 To release the stone from the knife, use a wooden spoon to carefully prise it away, then discard it.

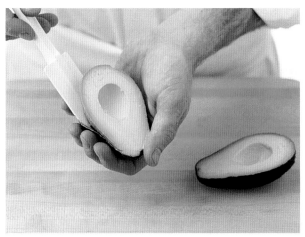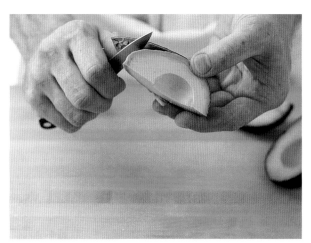

5 Use a spatula to remove the flesh from the skin, keeping it whole if possible. Then place the avocado on a chopping board and cut into slices or wedges.

6 Alternatively, quarter the avocado and hold it very gently to avoid damaging the flesh. Then use a small paring knife to peel away the skin.

7 To dice the avocado, cut it into neat slices lengthways, then repeat the cuts crossways to the desired size.

Storing avocado

Store the fruits in a **cool, dark place**, but do not chill. Once cut and exposed to oxygen, an avocado will discolour quickly. The easiest way to slow this process is by rubbing the exposed flesh with the cut side of a **lemon or lime wedge**. Lay a sheet of **cling film** over the top, pressing down as close to the flesh as possible, and store in a refrigerator until needed.

Techniques
Preparing peppers
Red, green, orange, and yellow peppers add colour to a dish.

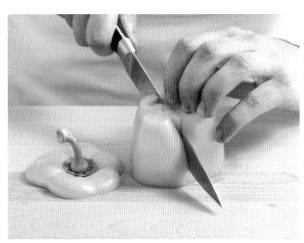

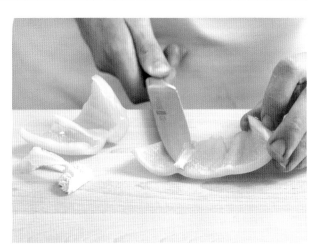

1 Place the pepper on its side. Cut off the top and bottom, then stand it on one of the cut ends and slice in half. Remove the core and seeds.

2 Lay each section flat. Remove the pale, fleshy ribs. Cut into smaller sections, following the divisions of the pepper, and chop as required.

Roasting and skinning peppers
Charring the skin makes peeling easier and lends a smoky flavour.

1 Use a pair of tongs to hold the pepper over a flame or place it under a hot grill to char the skin, turning occasionally. Cool in a plastic bag.

2 When it has cooled, peel away the skin. Pull off the stalk, with the core attached. Discard the seeds and dice the flesh or cut it into strips.

Preparing chillies

Removing the seeds and veins from chillies will reduce their heat.

1 Cut the chilli in half lengthways. Using the tip of your knife, scrape out the seeds and remove the membrane and stem.

2 Place the chilli half flesh-side down and flatten. Turn over and slice lengthways into strips. For dice, slice the strips crossways into equal pieces.

Roasting and grinding chillies

Remove the stems and seeds before dry-roasting the chillies.

1 To impart a smoky flavour to chillies, dry-roast in a heavy-based frying pan over a high heat. Remove when they begin to darken.

2 Use a mortar and pestle to grind dry-roasted chillies to a powder. Alternatively, they can be soaked, sieved, and ground to a paste.

Boiling green vegetables
Texture and colour are best preserved if the cooking is brief.

1 Bring a pan of salted water to the boil. Add the prepared vegetables. Bring to a rapid boil and cook until they are tender.

2 Drain through a colander and serve, or, to set the green colour and stop the vegetables cooking, rinse under cold running water.

Stir-frying vegetables
Speed is the key to successful stir-frying; toss and stir continuously.

1 When the wok (or pan) is hot, add sunflower, rapeseed, or groundnut oil, tilting the pan to spread the oil. Then toss in garlic or ginger.

2 Add the desired vegetables and toss them continuously. Add a couple of tablespoons of water, cover, and cook briefly until tender.

Steaming vegetables

As the vegetables are not immersed, nutrients are better preserved.

1 Bring 2.5cm (1in) of water to the boil in the bottom pan of a steamer. Place the prepared vegetables in the upper basket and position on top.

2 When the steam rises, cover the pan with a fitted lid and cook until the vegetables are just tender when pierced with a knife.

Sautéing firm vegetables

Use this quick method of cooking for batonettes or dice.

1 Set a sauté pan over a high heat. When hot, add a thin layer of oil. Once the oil is hot, add the vegetables and keep turning them to cook evenly.

2 Keep tossing the vegetables in the pan. Once they take on a light golden-brown colour and become tender, remove from the heat and serve.

Techniques
Preparing herbs
Fresh herbs can be used whole, chopped, or pounded.

To strip the leaves off woody herbs, hold the top end and run the thumb and forefinger of the other hand along the stalk.

For a bouquet garni, tie a sprig of thyme and parsley with a bay leaf. Rosemary or sage could also be used. Discard before serving.

Chopping tender herbs
Herbs with easily bruised leaves should be chopped bunched together.

1 To chop herbs with tender leaves, such as basil, without bruising them, stack the leaves together and roll them into a tight bunch.

2 Holding the bunch steady and using the knife in a rocking motion, chop finely, turning the leaves 90 degrees halfway through.

Preparing spices

Bruising, cutting, and grinding help to release the aroma of spices.

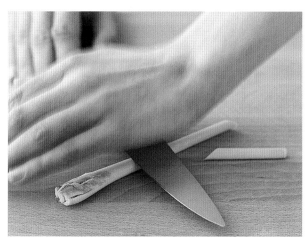

To prepare whole fresh spices such as lemongrass, bruise them by pressing down with the flat side of a heavy knife. This will help to release their volatile oils.

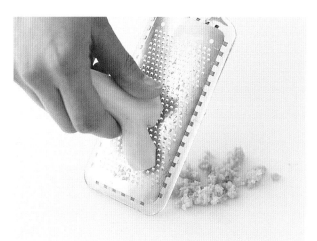

To prepare spice roots such as ginger, turmeric, and horseradish, grate them or finely chop them by hand, using a knife. Peel off the skin beforehand.

When spices are fried until lightly coloured, the oil takes on their flavour. It can then be used along with the spices.

To dry-roast spices, place them in an oven preheated to 160°C (325°F/Gas 3), or toast them in a dry pan until lightly browned.

The recipes

Every recipe in this book puts vegetables at the centre of the plate. You'll find delicious vegetable combinations and flavour pairings, as well as exciting ways to make the most of any vegetable by using a range of herbs, spices, nuts, pulses, and seeds.

Soups and salads

Gazpacho

SERVES 6–8 **PREPARATION** 30 MINS

Wonderfully refreshing, this is a perfect lunch for a hot summer day. **It's fantastically quick to make and healthy too.** Serve with garlic-rubbed toast.

INGREDIENTS

1 red pepper, deseeded
 and chopped
10 spring onions, chopped, or
 1 red onion, finely chopped
5 garlic cloves, chopped
1 cucumber, finely chopped
1kg (2¼lb) ripe tomatoes,
 finely chopped
1 tbsp chopped thyme,
 marjoram, parsley, mint,
 or basil
100g (3½oz) stale bread
1 chilli, deseeded and finely
 chopped, or ½ tsp cayenne
 pepper (optional)
2 tbsp red wine vinegar
3 tbsp olive oil, plus extra
 for drizzling
salt and freshly ground
 black pepper

1 Place a serving bowl in the fridge. Put the pepper, spring onions or onion, garlic, cucumber, and tomatoes in a mixing bowl, then add the herbs.

2 Whizz the bread in a blender to make breadcrumbs, then add to the mixing bowl along with the chilli or cayenne pepper, if using, vinegar, and oil. Gradually add 100ml (3½fl oz) chilled water to give it a nice thick consistency; use more if preferred.

3 Transfer to the blender and, depending on your preference, either whizz briefly so that the odd chunk of cucumber remains or blend the soup until smooth. Season generously with salt and pepper. Transfer to the serving bowl, add a few ice cubes, and drizzle with oil.

Borscht

SERVES 4   PREPARATION **15 MINS**   TO COOK **1 HR 30 MINS**

This thickly textured, satisfying soup is a Russian classic that can be enjoyed at any time of year. Try it with grated carrot piled on top and hunks of dark rye bread.

1 Melt the butter in a large saucepan over a medium heat. Add the beetroot, onion, carrot, and celery. Cook, stirring, for 5 minutes, or until just softened. Add the tomatoes and garlic, if using, and cook for 2–3 minutes, stirring frequently, then stir in the stock.

2 Tie the bay leaves and cloves in a small piece of muslin or new disposable kitchen cloth and add to the pan. Bring the soup to the boil, then lower the heat, cover, and simmer for 1 hour 20 minutes. Discard the muslin bag, stir in the lemon juice, and season to taste with salt and pepper. Ladle the soup into warmed bowls and add a swirl of soured cream to each one.

INGREDIENTS

45g (1½oz) butter or goose fat
2 large beetroot, grated
1 onion, roughly grated
1 carrot, roughly grated
1 celery stick, roughly grated
400g can chopped tomatoes
1 garlic clove, crushed
   (optional)
1.7 litres (3 pints) hot
   vegetable stock
2 bay leaves
4 cloves
2 tbsp lemon juice
salt and freshly ground
   black pepper
200ml (7fl oz) soured cream

French red onion soup with brandy and Gruyère croûtes

SERVES 4   PREPARATION **10 MINS**   TO COOK **40 MINS**

Rich and full of flavour, onion soup cannot be beaten on a cold day. Red onions add colour and are sweeter and more intensely flavoured than brown onions.

INGREDIENTS

60g (2oz) butter

4 large red onions, quartered and thinly sliced

2 tbsp soft light brown sugar

1 litre (1¾ pints) vegetable stock

2 tbsp brandy

salt and freshly ground black pepper

8 diagonal slices of baguette

175g (6oz) Gruyère cheese, grated

1 Melt the butter in a large saucepan. Add the onions and fry, stirring, for 2 minutes. Cover, reduce the heat to low, and cook gently for 10 minutes until really soft, shaking the pan occasionally.

2 Increase the heat, add the sugar, and fry, stirring continuously, for 5 minutes or until richly browned (but take care not to burn). Add the stock, brandy, and a little salt and pepper. Bring to the boil, reduce the heat, and simmer gently for 15 minutes.

3 Meanwhile, make the croûtes. Preheat the grill and toast the bread on both sides. When ready to serve, add the cheese to the croûtes and grill until just melted and sizzling.

4 Ladle the soup into warmed bowls and float 2 cheese croûtes on each. Add a grinding of pepper and serve immediately.

Cheese, red pepper, and sweetcorn chowder

SERVES 4   **PREPARATION** **15 MINS**   **TO COOK** **35 MINS**

When time is short, use a large can of sweetcorn with peppers instead of the corn cobs and pepper. Simmering the cobs in the stock is not essential.

INGREDIENTS

2 large sweetcorn cobs
1 litre (1¾ pints)
   vegetable stock
knob of butter
1 onion, finely chopped
1 potato, peeled and
   finely diced
1 red pepper, deseeded
   and finely chopped
1 bouquet garni
3 tbsp cornflour
150ml (5fl oz) milk
115g (4oz) strong Cheddar
   cheese, grated
2 tbsp chopped parsley,
   plus extra to garnish
salt and freshly ground
   black pepper

1 Remove the sweetcorn kernels from the cobs (see p39). Put the stripped cobs in a saucepan with the stock. Bring to the boil, cover, and simmer gently for 5 minutes to extract the flavour. Strain the stock into a bowl and discard the cobs.

2 In the same saucepan, melt the butter and fry the onion gently, stirring, for 2 minutes until softened, but not browned. Add the reserved stock, all the prepared vegetables, and the bouquet garni. Bring to the boil, then reduce the heat, partially cover, and simmer gently for 15 minutes until the vegetables are soft. Discard the bouquet garni.

3 Blend the cornflour with the milk and stir into the soup. Bring back to the boil and simmer, stirring, for 1 minute until slightly thickened. Stir in the cheese until melted, add the parsley, then season with salt and pepper to taste. Ladle into bowls and sprinkle with a little extra chopped parsley.

Leek, barley, and root vegetable broth with basil oil

SERVES 4–6   **PREPARATION 10 MINS**   TO COOK **45 MINS**

Barley adds substance to this delicate soup. For a more filling meal and extra protein, add a 410g can of haricot beans and an extra 200ml (7fl oz) vegetable stock.

INGREDIENTS

200ml (7fl oz) dry white wine
1.5 litres (2¾ pints)
   vegetable stock
75g (2½oz) pearl barley
1 onion, chopped
2 carrots, finely diced
½ small swede, finely diced
1 potato, peeled and
   finely diced
1 turnip, finely diced
1 large bay leaf
2 star anise
salt and freshly ground
   black pepper
crusty bread, to serve

For the basil oil
handful of basil leaves,
   roughly chopped
4 tbsp olive oil

1 Put the white wine in a large saucepan and bring to the boil. Boil rapidly for 2–3 minutes until reduced by half.

2 Add the remaining soup ingredients. Bring to the boil, then reduce the heat, cover, and simmer gently for 40 minutes until the barley is tender. Discard the bay leaf and star anise. Taste and adjust the seasoning.

3 To make the basil oil, blend the basil with the oil in a blender or small food processor.

4 Ladle the soup into warmed bowls. Drizzle the basil oil on top of each and serve with crusty bread.

Four ways with Mushrooms

Mushroom soup ▷

TAKES 55 mins **SERVES** 4

Melt 30g (1oz) **butter** in a large saucepan, add 1 finely chopped **onion**, 2 finely chopped **celery sticks**, and 1 crushed **garlic clove**, and fry for 3–4 minutes, or until softened. Stir in 450g (1lb) roughly chopped **mixed mushrooms** and continue to fry for 5–6 minutes. Add 200g (7oz) peeled and diced **potatoes** and 1 litre (1¾ pints) **vegetable stock** and bring to the boil. Reduce the heat and simmer gently for 30 minutes. Use a hand-held blender to whizz the soup until smooth, in batches if necessary. Sprinkle in 2 tbsp finely chopped **parsley**, season with **salt** and freshly ground **black pepper**, and serve.

◁ Tofu and mushroom stroganoff

TAKES 35 mins **SERVES** 4

Heat 1 tbsp **sunflower oil** in a pan. Stir-fry 350g (12oz) diced **tofu** over a high heat until golden. Set aside. Add 1 tbsp oil, reduce the heat, and fry 1 sliced **red onion** and 2 crushed **garlic cloves** until soft. Add 1 **red** and 1 **orange pepper**, sliced, and 250g (9oz) **mixed mushrooms**, quartered. Stir-fry for 5 minutes. Add 2 tbsp each **tomato purée** and **smooth peanut butter** and the tofu. Stir in 150ml (5fl oz) **vegetable stock** and 2 tsp **cornflour** mixed to a paste with water. Cook for 3 minutes. Add 200g (7oz) **crème fraîche** and **salt** and freshly ground **black pepper**. Simmer for 2 minutes, sprinkle with **chives**, and serve with **rice**.

Mushrooms come in a range of flavours, from the mild button type to full-bodied portobellos and nutty chanterelles. **All should be firm and earthy-smelling.** Always wipe them – but don't wash them – before use.

Mushrooms in garlic sauce ▷

TAKES 25 mins **SERVES** 4

Heat 4 tbsp **olive oil** in a frying pan. Add 400g (14oz) **chestnut mushrooms**, halved, 4 finely sliced **garlic cloves**, and 2 **red chillies**, deseeded and finely sliced. Fry for 2 minutes over a low heat. Add 4 tbsp **dry sherry**, crumble in 1 **vegetable stock** cube, and season with freshly ground **black pepper**. Cook over a medium heat for 10 minutes, or until the mushrooms have released their juices. Cook for a further 3 minutes, or until the juices have reduced by half, and then serve with some fresh **crusty bread**.

◁ Mushroom bruschetta

TAKES 30 mins **SERVES** 12

Preheat the oven to 180°C (350°F/Gas 4). Brush 12 slices of **ciabatta** with **olive oil**, then bake for 10 minutes. Melt 60g (2oz) **butter** in a pan, add 4 finely chopped **shallots** and 2 finely chopped **garlic cloves**, and fry gently for 5 minutes. Add 450g (1lb) sliced **field mushrooms** and fry until wilted. Add 4 tbsp **Marsala**, bring to the boil, then simmer until reduced to 1 tsp. Reduce the heat, add 100ml (3½fl oz) **double cream**, and simmer for 5 minutes. Add **salt** and freshly ground **black pepper**, and stir in 2 tbsp finely chopped **parsley** and 3 tbsp grated **Parmesan cheese**. Spoon the mixture over the toasted bread.

Aubergine, courgette, and flageolet salad with mozzarella and red pesto dressing

SERVES 4–6   **PREPARATION 10 MINS**   **TO COOK 25 MINS**

Serve this colourful salad as a **light lunch for four or as a starter for six**. To prepare the onion, cut it into thin slices, discarding the ends, before peeling off the outer layer.

INGREDIENTS

2 small aubergines

2 courgettes

7 tbsp olive oil

400g can flageolet beans, rinsed and drained

1 garlic clove, crushed

salt and freshly ground black pepper

1–2 tbsp lime juice

115g (4oz) cherry tomatoes, halved

1 small red onion, thinly sliced

4 tbsp red pesto

125g (4½oz) ball fresh mozzarella cheese, torn

a few pimento-stuffed green olives, halved

crusty bread, to serve

1 Preheat a griddle pan. Trim the aubergines and courgettes and cut lengthways into 5mm (¼in) slices. Brush with some of the oil. Cook in batches on a hot griddle for 3 minutes on each side, pressing down with a fish slice, until tender and striped brown. Wrap in foil to keep warm and set aside.

2 Put the flageolet beans in a large saucepan. Drizzle with 2 tbsp oil and add the garlic, salt and pepper, and lime juice (leaving a little for the pesto), to taste. Heat through, stirring gently, then remove from the heat. Add the tomatoes and onion slices and toss gently.

3 Thin the pesto with 4 tbsp oil, or enough to form a spoonable dressing. Taste and sharpen with lime juice.

4 Gently mix the aubergines and courgettes into the beans. The mixture should now be just warm.

5 Stir in the mozzarella, then spoon the salad into serving bowls. Drizzle the pesto dressing over and scatter with the olives. Serve with crusty bread.

Thai vegetable salad with cabbage and peanuts

SERVES 4 **PREPARATION 15 MINS**

This is a simpler version of the Thai salad som tam, which has a hot, salty, sweet, and sour dressing. Add some cooled rice noodles to turn it into a main course.

INGREDIENTS

2 dessert apples
4 carrots, grated
1 small white cabbage, shredded
handful of sunflower seeds
handful of salted or dry-roasted peanuts

For the dressing
2 tbsp light soy sauce
1 green chilli, deseeded and finely chopped
1 garlic clove, grated
juice of 2 limes
1–2 tsp caster sugar
handful of coriander, finely chopped

1 To make the dressing, put all the dressing ingredients in a small bowl and mix thoroughly until the sugar has dissolved. Taste to check the flavour – if it needs sweetening, add more sugar, and if it needs saltiness, add a little more soy sauce.

2 Quarter and core the apples, then chop into bite-sized pieces. Put in a bowl with the carrot, cabbage, and sunflower seeds. Mix together thoroughly.

3 Drizzle the dressing over and toss together so that everything is well mixed. Transfer to a serving dish and scatter the peanuts over.

Squash with cranberries and chestnuts

SERVES 4   **PREPARATION 10 MINS**   TO COOK **30 MINS**

This gently spiced, flavoursome dish makes excellent use of seasonal ingredients for a warm winter salad. It is also good served as a side dish.

1 Heat the oil and butter in a large frying pan. Add the allspice, cinnamon, and squash. Season well with salt and pepper and cook over a low-medium heat, stirring occasionally, for 15 minutes, or until the squash begins to soften a little. Add a little more oil, if needed.

2 Add the chestnuts and stir so that they are coated with the oil. Cook over a low heat for 5–10 minutes, then add the cranberries and cook for a further 5 minutes.

3 Taste and season again, if needed, adding a little sugar if the cranberries are too tart (cook until the sugar has dissolved).

4 Pile a bed of rocket and watercress on a shallow dish and scatter the squash mixture over it. Serve warm.

INGREDIENTS

1–2 tbsp extra virgin olive oil
knob of butter
pinch of ground allspice
pinch of ground cinnamon
1 butternut squash, peeled, halved, deseeded, and cut into bite-sized pieces
salt and freshly ground black pepper
240g can ready-cooked chestnuts
50g (1¾oz) cranberries
sugar, to taste (optional)
100g (3½oz) mixed rocket and watercress

Warm pasta, kale, and duck egg salad with truffle oil

SERVES 4   PREPARATION **20 MINS**   TO COOK **10 MINS**

If fresh wild mushrooms aren't available, use 140g (5oz) white or chestnut ones, thickly sliced, and a handful of dried **morels, chanterelles, or porcini,** reconstituted.

INGREDIENTS

4 large duck eggs, scrubbed
salt and freshly ground
   black pepper
225g (8oz) conchiglie pasta
200g (7oz) finely shredded
   curly kale, thick
   stalks removed
knob of butter
2 tbsp olive oil
200g (7oz) mixed wild
   mushrooms, cut up if large
2 tbsp chopped thyme,
   plus a few thyme leaves,
   to garnish
2 spring onions, chopped
4 tbsp truffle oil
2 tbsp white balsamic
   condiment
small black truffle, grated
   (optional), to garnish
warm ciabatta bread, to serve

1 Place the duck eggs in a steamer basket or large metal colander. Fill a bowl with cold water and set near the hob.

2 Add a generous pinch of salt to a large pan of water and bring to the boil, then add the pasta and stir. Bring back to the boil, top with the steamer containing the eggs, cover, and cook for 5 minutes. Add the kale to the steamer, cover, and cook for a further 5 minutes. Quickly take the steamer off the pan and immediately put the eggs in the bowl of cold water. Drain the pasta and rinse with cold water. Drain again and return to the pan.

3 While the kale is cooking, melt the butter and olive oil in a frying pan. Add the mushrooms and thyme and sauté, stirring, for 3 minutes. Season with salt and pepper. Add to the pasta with the kale and spring onions.

4 Whisk 2 tbsp truffle oil into the juices in the mushroom pan, along with the balsamic condiment, and a pinch of salt and a good grinding of pepper. Heat through, stirring, then pour into the pasta mixture. Toss gently.

5 Pile into dishes and drizzle with the remaining truffle oil. Carefully shell the duck eggs and place one on top of each salad. Cut open so that the yolk trickles out slightly. Add a grating of black truffle, if using, and a few thyme leaves. Serve with warm ciabatta.

Pasta, noodles, and rice

Farfalle with spinach, avocado, baby plum tomatoes, and pumpkin seeds

SERVES 4   **PREPARATION 10 MINS**   **TO COOK 16 MINS**

Available in vacuum packs, slow-roasted tomatoes are soft yet intensely flavoured. Semi-dried or sun-dried tomatoes, drained of oil, may be used instead.

INGREDIENTS

400g (14oz) dried farfalle pasta
2 tbsp olive oil
4 spring onions, cut into
   short lengths
1 garlic clove, finely chopped
1 tsp crushed dried chillies
350g (12oz) baby
   spinach leaves
150ml (5fl oz) vegetable stock
4 slow-roasted
   tomatoes, chopped
175g (6oz) baby plum
   tomatoes, halved
30g (1oz) pitted black
   olives, sliced
1½ tbsp capers
2 avocados, peeled, stoned,
   and diced
squeeze of lemon juice
salt and freshly ground
   black pepper
3 tbsp pumpkin seeds
lemon wedges and a few torn
   basil leaves, to garnish

1 Cook the pasta according to the packet instructions. Drain. Heat the oil in a deep-sided sauté pan or wok. Add the spring onions and garlic and fry, stirring gently, for 1 minute. Stir in the chillies.

2 Add the spinach and stock and simmer, turning over gently for about 2 minutes until beginning to wilt. Gently fold in the pasta and the remaining ingredients. Simmer for 3 minutes until most of the liquid has been absorbed.

3 Pile into warmed, shallow bowls. Garnish with lemon wedges and a few torn basil leaves.

Pasta with butternut squash, chilli, and Parmesan cheese

SERVES 4   PREPARATION **20 MINS**   TO COOK **30 MINS**

Ripening pumpkins and squashes herald the onset of autumn. Perfect for those slightly cooler days, **this dish has the comfort of cream and the warmth of red chillies.**

INGREDIENTS

3 tbsp olive oil
200g (7oz) butternut squash, halved, deseeded, peeled and diced
salt and freshly ground black pepper
1 garlic clove, crushed
½ red chilli, deseeded and finely chopped
8 sage leaves
150ml (5fl oz) single cream
25g (scant 1oz) Parmesan cheese, grated, plus extra to serve
350g (12oz) conchiglie pasta

1 Heat 2 tbsp oil in a frying pan, add the squash, and toss in the oil. Add 3 tbsp water and some salt and pepper. Bring to the boil and reduce the heat to as low as possible. Cover and cook very gently for 10 minutes until soft, stirring occasionally. Leave to cool for a few minutes. Meanwhile, gently fry the garlic, chilli, and sage in a little oil for 2–3 minutes.

2 Once the squash has cooled slightly, put it into a blender or food processor. Add the cream and Parmesan, the cooked garlic, chilli, and sage mixture, and a little salt and plenty of pepper. Blend it all to a fine purée, adding 1–2 tbsp water if it looks too thick.

3 Cook the pasta until it is cooked but still has a bit of bite to it – al dente – and drain it. Quickly reheat the sauce in the pasta pan, adding more water if it seems a little stiff. Put the pasta back into the pan and mix it well, allowing the sauce to coat the pasta. Serve with plenty of fresh Parmesan.

Ricotta and squash ravioli

SERVES 4   **PREPARATION 1 HOUR, PLUS CHILLING**   **TO COOK 4–5 MINS**

You can make the ravioli a day in advance, if you wish. Dust them with polenta, layer in a sealable plastic box with oiled cling film in between, cover, and chill.

1 Sift the flour into a bowl. Make a well in the centre and add the eggs. Gradually mix together to form a dough. Knead gently on a lightly floured surface for about 5 minutes until smooth and elastic. Wrap in cling film and chill for at least 30 minutes.

2 To make the ravioli filling, cook the squash as for the pasta dish on the opposite page. Cool slightly, then blitz until smooth in a food processor. Leave to cool. Place the ricotta, Parmesan, garlic, and nutmeg in a bowl. Stir in the squash and season with salt and pepper. Chill.

3 Roll out the pasta dough very thinly on a lightly floured surface. Cut out 76–80 rounds using a 6cm (2½in) round fluted cutter, re-kneading and rolling the trimmings as necessary. Place ½ heaped tsp of filling on half the rounds. Brush the other rounds with water, place on top, dampened sides down, and pinch the edges together to seal. This will make 38–40 ravioli. Dust with polenta to prevent them from sticking together. Cover and chill until required.

4 Bring a large pan of salted water to the boil. Add the pasta and cook for 4–5 minutes, or until al dente. Drain and return to the pan.

5 For the sage butter, heat the oil, butter, lemon zest, and sage together, stirring until the butter melts, and season with plenty of pepper. Add to the pasta and toss well to mix. Serve in shallow bowls, sprinkled with some grated Parmesan.

INGREDIENTS

225g (8oz) tipo "00" pasta
  flour (or fine plain flour)
3 eggs, beaten
plain flour, for dusting
polenta, for dusting

For the filling

1 tbsp olive oil
175g (6oz) butternut squash,
  halved, deseeded, peeled
  and diced
salt and freshly ground
  black pepper
85g (3oz) ricotta cheese
30g (1oz) Parmesan cheese,
  grated, plus extra to serve
1 garlic clove, crushed
½ tsp grated nutmeg

For the sage butter

3 tbsp olive oil
60g (2oz) butter
grated zest of ½ lemon
2 tsp roughly chopped
  sage leaves

Pumpkin, spinach, and Gorgonzola lasagne

SERVES 4   **PREPARATION 25–30 MINS**   TO COOK **1–1¼ HRS**

This vegetable lasagne is **rich and satisfying, with fresh sage and nutmeg bringing the flavours alive**. If pumpkin is not available, use butternut squash or sweet potato.

INGREDIENTS

small pumpkin or butternut squash (approx. 800g/1¾lb) peeled, halved, deseeded, and chopped into bite-sized pieces
1 tbsp olive oil
salt and freshly ground black pepper
8 sage leaves, roughly chopped
pinch of grated nutmeg
pinch of dried chilli flakes (optional)
pinch of allspice
200g (7oz) spinach
10 pre-cooked lasagne sheets
125g (4½oz) Gorgonzola cheese, chopped
lightly dressed green salad, to serve

For the sauce
60g (2oz) butter
60g (2oz) plain flour
900ml (1½ pints) milk
1 bay leaf

1 Preheat the oven to 200°C (400°F/Gas 6). Place the pumpkin in a large roasting tin, add the oil and plenty of salt and pepper, and toss to coat; the tin must be large or the pumpkin will steam rather than roast. Sprinkle over the sage, nutmeg, chilli, if using, and allspice and stir. Roast for 20–30 minutes, stirring halfway, until golden, then remove. Stir in the spinach, which will wilt in a few minutes. Set aside. Reduce the oven temperature to 190°C (375°F/Gas 5).

2 For the sauce, melt the butter in a medium pan. Remove from the heat and blend in the flour. Gradually blend in the milk, stirring continuously with a wooden spoon or wire whisk. Add the bay leaf. Return to the heat and bring to the boil, stirring all the time until thickened, then cook for 2 minutes, continuing to stir as before. Add salt and pepper to taste, discard the bay leaf, and set aside.

3 Spoon half the pumpkin mixture into a 20 × 30cm (8 × 12in) ovenproof dish. Seasoning well between each layer, add half the lasagne sheets, half the sauce, and half the Gorgonzola. Repeat to use up all the ingredients. Place on a baking tray and bake for 30–40 minutes until golden and bubbling. Serve with a green salad.

Mixed mushroom and pak choi stir-fry with soba noodles

SERVES 4   PREPARATION **10 MINS**   TO COOK **8 MINS**

This dish uses cultivated mushrooms that originate from Japan. They are widely available in supermarkets, but chestnut mushrooms can be substituted if necessary.

INGREDIENTS

250g (9oz) dried soba or
  brown udon noodles
6 tbsp tamari or light
  soy sauce
1 tbsp lemon juice
2 tsp grated fresh root ginger
2 garlic cloves, crushed
1 tsp chopped lemongrass
  or lemongrass purée
1 tbsp caster sugar
¼–½ tsp wasabi paste
225g (8oz) fresh shelled
  or frozen soya beans
3 tbsp sunflower oil
1 bunch of spring onions,
  trimmed and sliced
2 celery sticks, cut
  into matchsticks
100g (3½oz) shiitake
  mushrooms, sliced
100g (3½oz) oyster
  mushrooms, sliced
100g (3½oz) enoki
  mushrooms, trimmed
  of base and separated
2 heads pak choi (approx.
  200g/7oz), coarsely shredded
2 tbsp sesame seeds,
  to garnish

1 Cook the noodles according to the packet instructions. Drain and set aside.

2 Whisk the tamari sauce, lemon juice, ginger, garlic, lemongrass, sugar, and wasabi paste in a small bowl with 2 tbsp water and set aside. Boil the soya beans in water for 3 minutes. Drain and set aside.

3 Heat the oil in a large frying pan or wok. Add the spring onions and celery and stir-fry for 2 minutes. Add all the mushrooms and stir-fry for 3 minutes. Add the pak choi and soya beans and stir-fry for 1 minute.

4 Add the noodles and the bowl of tamari sauce. Toss until everything is hot through and coated. Spoon into bowls and sprinkle with sesame seeds before serving.

Pasta, noodles, and rice
Thai noodle stir-fry

SERVES 4 **PREPARATION 15 MINS** **TO COOK 20 MINS**

Perfect in stir-fries, oriental greens add colour and a fresh flavour to the finished dish. The rice noodles used here are quite delicate – be careful not to overcook them.

INGREDIENTS

175g (6oz) dried thin
  rice noodles
3 tbsp sunflower oil
1 onion, sliced
1 stalk of lemongrass, outer
  leaves removed, woody end
  trimmed, and finely chopped
1 tsp finely grated fresh
  root ginger
1 red chilli, deseeded and
  finely chopped
1 orange pepper, deseeded
  and sliced
115g (4oz) sugarsnap
  peas, trimmed
225g (8oz) shiitake
  mushrooms, sliced
3 heads pak choi, shredded
3 tbsp light soy sauce
1 tsp sweet chilli sauce

1 Soak the noodles in a bowl of boiling water until softened, or as directed on the packet. Drain and set aside.

2 Heat the oil in a wok and stir-fry the onion for 2–3 minutes. Add the lemongrass, ginger, chilli, pepper, sugarsnap peas, and mushrooms, and stir-fry for 2 minutes.

3 Add the pak choi and stir-fry for a further 2 minutes, then add the noodles. Pour in the soy sauce and sweet chilli sauce. Toss everything together over the heat for 2–3 minutes, or until piping hot. Serve at once.

Split pea, noodle, and vegetable pot

SERVES 4   **PREPARATION 15 MINS**   TO COOK **1 HR**

The split peas will gradually absorb all the wonderful flavours of the spices, herbs, and coconut in this simple-to-cook noodle dish.

1 Soak the noodles in boiling water for 5 minutes, or as directed on the packet, then drain and set aside.

2 Heat the oil in a large, heavy-based pan. Add the onion and cook on a low heat for 2–3 minutes. Season well with salt and pepper. Stir in the garlic, turmeric, and coriander and cook for 2 minutes.

3 Add the carrots and courgettes, turn to coat, and cook for 5 minutes. Stir in the split peas and add the coconut milk. Increase the heat and allow to bubble for 1 minute, then add the stock and bring to the boil.

4 Reduce to a simmer and cook on a low heat, partially covered, for 40–50 minutes, or until the split peas begin to soften. Top up with hot water as needed – there should be plenty of liquid. Add the noodles for the last 5 minutes of cooking to heat through. Season well and serve garnished with the chopped coriander.

INGREDIENTS

85g (3oz) dried thin rice noodles
1 tbsp olive oil
1 onion, finely chopped
salt and freshly ground black pepper
2 garlic cloves, finely chopped
1 tsp turmeric
1 tsp coriander seeds, crushed
3 carrots, diced
2 courgettes, diced
225g (8oz) yellow split peas, rinsed
200ml (7fl oz) coconut milk
1 litre (1¾ pints) hot vegetable stock
large handful of coriander leaves, roughly chopped, to garnish

Vegetable ramen noodle bowl

SERVES 4   PREPARATION **10 MINS, PLUS SOAKING**   TO COOK **10 MINS**

Miso paste enhances the flavour of this dish, but omit it if preferred and season with more tamari. **Use dashi powder to make the vegetable stock,** if it is available.

INGREDIENTS

2 × 10cm (4in) pieces wakame

2 heaped tbsp dried
shiitake mushrooms

250g (9oz) dried ramen
noodles (or brown
rice noodles)

1 litre (1¾ pints)
vegetable stock

2 tbsp tamari or light soy sauce

2 tsp soft light brown sugar

3 tbsp mirin (or dry sherry)

4 spring onions, chopped

1 red pepper, deseeded
and finely sliced

2 heads of pak choi, cut
into thick shreds

1 courgette, cut into
matchsticks

4 radishes, sliced

225g can bamboo
shoots, drained

1 tsp crushed dried
chillies (optional)

1 tbsp red miso paste

250g block firm tofu,
cut into 8 slices

sweet chilli sauce, to drizzle

1 Soak the wakame and mushrooms in 300ml (10fl oz) warm water for 30 minutes. Lift out the wakame and cut out any thick stalks, if necessary. If the wakame is large, cut into pieces before returning to the soaking water with the mushrooms.

2 Cook the noodles according to the packet instructions. Drain. Put the stock in a large saucepan with the remaining ingredients, except the miso paste and tofu. Add the wakame, mushrooms, and soaking water. Bring to the boil, reduce the heat, and simmer for 3 minutes.

3 Blend a ladleful of the stock with the miso paste until smooth. Pour back into the pan and stir gently. Taste and add more tamari, if necessary. Make sure the soup is very hot, but not boiling.

4 Divide the noodles among 4 large open soup bowls. Add 2 slices of tofu to each bowl and ladle the very hot soup over. Serve at once with sweet chilli sauce to drizzle over, if using.

Fiery peanut and pepper noodles

SERVES 4   PREPARATION **20 MINS**   TO COOK **4–5 MINS**

This is **a great meal to put together in a hurry**. If fresh noodles aren't to hand, use 250g (9oz) dried noodles, reconstituted according to packet instructions.

INGREDIENTS

1 red pepper
1 green pepper
1 tbsp sunflower oil
4 spring onions, chopped
1 garlic clove, finely chopped
1 courgette, finely chopped
1–2 green jalapeño chillies,
   deseeded and chopped
1 tsp grated root ginger
1 tbsp chopped
   flat-leaf parsley
1 tbsp chopped coriander,
   plus a few torn leaves,
   to garnish
grated zest and juice of 1 lime
4 tbsp crunchy peanut butter
3 tbsp soy sauce
1 tbsp dry sherry
500g (1lb 2oz) fresh
   egg noodles
60g (2oz) roasted peanuts,
   chopped, to garnish

1 Grill the peppers for about 15 minutes, turning once or twice, until blackened in places. Put in a plastic bag and leave until cold. Rub off the skins and dice the flesh, discarding the stalk and seeds.

2 Heat the oil in a wok or large frying pan. Add the spring onions, garlic, and courgette, and stir-fry for 1 minute. Add the peppers, chillies, ginger, herbs, lime zest and juice, peanut butter, soy sauce, sherry, and 9 tbsp water. Stir until the peanut butter melts. Add the noodles, then toss for 2 minutes until piping hot. Pile into warmed bowls and sprinkle with peanuts and a few torn coriander leaves.

Pasta, noodles, and rice
Mushroom orzotto

SERVES 4   **PREPARATION 10 MINS, PLUS SOAKING**   TO COOK **45 MINS**

Barley makes a fabulous, risotto-type dish that is easy to cook. Unlike rice, **it can produce a creamy, nutty-textured result with the liquid added all in one go**.

1 Soak the dried mushrooms in boiling water for 30 minutes until tender. Drain, chop, and set aside.

2 In a pan, soften the onion and garlic in the butter, stirring, for 2 minutes. Add the fresh mushrooms and wine. Simmer for 2 minutes. Stir in the barley and thyme. Add the stock and season with salt and pepper. Bring to the boil, then simmer for about 40 minutes, stirring twice, until the barley is tender, but with a bit of bite, and the liquid is almost absorbed.

3 Add the chopped mushrooms and cream to the mixture and heat through, but do not boil. Garnish with thyme leaves and serve with the Parmesan cheese.

INGREDIENTS

1 tbsp dried mushrooms
1 onion, chopped
1 garlic clove, crushed
15g (½oz) butter
225g (8oz) chestnut
    mushrooms, sliced
150ml (5fl oz) dry white wine
200g (7oz) pearl barley
2 tsp chopped thyme, plus
    a few leaves, to garnish
750ml (1¼ pints)
    vegetable stock
salt and freshly ground
    black pepper
2–3 tbsp single cream
Parmesan cheese, grated,
    to serve

Cashew nut paella

SERVES 4   PREPARATION **10 MINS**   TO COOK **25 MINS**

Cashews are expensive nuts, but they make a delicious paella. Try substituting chopped cooked chestnuts or even toasted hazelnuts for a change.

INGREDIENTS

large pinch of saffron strands
750ml (1¼ pints) hot
    vegetable stock
2 tbsp olive oil
1 leek, chopped
1 onion, chopped
2 garlic cloves, crushed
1 red pepper, deseeded
    and chopped
1 carrot, chopped
250g (9oz) paella rice
150ml (5fl oz) dry white wine
115g (4oz) chestnut
    mushrooms, sliced
115g (4oz) roasted, unsalted
    cashew nuts
salt and freshly ground
    black pepper
115g (4oz) fresh shelled
    or frozen peas
1½ tbsp chopped thyme
4 tomatoes, quartered
½ tsp smoked paprika
sprig of flat-leaf parsley and
    lemon wedges, to garnish
crusty bread and green
    salad, to serve

1 Put the saffron in the stock to infuse. Heat the oil in a paella pan or large frying pan and fry the leek, onion, garlic, red pepper, and carrot, stirring, for 3 minutes until softened, but not browned. Add the rice and stir until coated in oil and glistening.

2 Add the wine and boil until it has been absorbed, stirring. Stir in the saffron-infused stock, mushrooms, nuts, and some salt and pepper. Bring to the boil, stirring once, then reduce the heat, cover, and simmer very gently for 10 minutes.

3 Add the peas and thyme, stir gently, then distribute the tomatoes over the top. Cover and simmer very gently for a further 10 minutes until the rice is just tender and has absorbed most of the liquid, but is still creamy.

4 Sprinkle the paprika over and stir through gently, taking care not to break up the tomatoes. Taste and adjust the seasoning, if necessary.

5 Garnish with a sprig of parsley and lemon wedges and serve hot with crusty bread and a green salad.

Pan-fries
and fritters

Chinese pumpkin fritters

MAKES 20   **PREPARATION 15 MINS, PLUS CHILLING**   TO COOK **40 MINS**

These crisp, bite-sized fritters, fried in a beer batter, make a light supper accompanied by rice. Use only plain flour for the batter, if preferred.

INGREDIENTS

500g (1lb 2oz) pumpkin or
   butternut squash, peeled,
   halved, seeded, and grated
5cm (2in) piece fresh root
   ginger, grated
½ tsp turmeric
1 red chilli, deseeded and
   finely chopped
1 tbsp plain flour, plus extra
   for dusting
salt and freshly ground
   black pepper
sunflower oil, for deep-frying
soy sauce and rice, to serve

For the batter
100ml (3½fl oz) beer
50g (1¾oz) plain flour
50g (1¾oz) gram
   (chickpea) flour
3 tbsp sparkling water

1 Put the pumpkin in a colander or steamer basket and sit it over a pan of simmering water, covered, for 10–15 minutes until the pumpkin is tender. Remove, leave to cool slightly, then squeeze out any excess water. Place in a bowl and mix in the ginger, turmeric, chilli, and plain flour. Season with salt and pepper.

2 Dust your hands with flour, then take a tablespoonful of the pumpkin mixture and shape it into a ball. Repeat to make 19 more round balls. Place them on a lightly floured baking tray and chill in the refrigerator for at least 30 minutes to firm.

3 For the batter, place all the ingredients in a bowl and season. Stir until combined, but still lumpy. If the batter is thin, add more of the flours in equal amounts – it should be the consistency of thick cream.

4 Pour the oil to a depth of 5cm (2in) into a wok or a large, deep-sided, non-stick frying pan and place over a medium-high heat until hot. Don't leave the wok or pan unattended. Take off the heat when not using, and keep a fire blanket nearby in case of emergency.

5 Dip the pumpkin balls into the batter one at a time, making sure they are well coated. Fry them in the hot oil, about 5 at a time, cooking each side for 2–3 minutes until golden and crisp. Remove and place on kitchen paper to drain. Serve with a small bowl of soy sauce and some rice.

Pan-fries and fritters

Sweetcorn fritters with tomato salsa

SERVES 4   PREPARATION **20 MINS**   TO COOK **10 MINS**

If you're lucky enough to obtain **newly harvested sweetcorn**, there is no need to blanch it – the kernels will be sweet and tender enough used fresh.

1 If using fresh sweetcorn, remove the husks and silk and cut off the kernels (see p39). Blanch the kernels in boiling water for 3 minutes. Drain, rinse with cold water, and drain again.

2 Sift the flour and baking powder into a bowl. Mix the eggs and milk together in a jug and gradually whisk them into the flour to make a thick batter. Add the corn, paprika, the white parts of the spring onions, 2 tbsp coriander, and the chilli, if using. Mix well and season with salt and pepper.

3 Heat the sunflower oil in a large frying pan and add the batter mixture a tablespoonful at a time. Use the back of the spoon to spread the fritters out slightly, and fry for 2–3 minutes on each side until puffed up and golden brown. Fry in batches until all the mixture is cooked, adding a little more sunflower oil if necessary.

4 Put the tomatoes, the remaining coriander and spring onion, the olive oil, and the Tabasco or chilli sauce into a food processor or blender, and process until blended but still quite chunky. Check the salsa for seasoning. Serve the hot fritters with the salsa on the side.

INGREDIENTS

2 large sweetcorn cobs, or 250g (9oz) fresh or frozen kernels
100g (3½oz) self-raising flour
1 tsp baking powder
2 large eggs
4 tbsp milk
1 tsp smoked paprika
2 spring onions, finely chopped, green and white parts separated
4 tbsp chopped coriander
1 red chilli, deseeded and finely chopped (optional)
salt and freshly ground black pepper
2 tbsp sunflower oil
2 ripe tomatoes, skinned and roughly chopped
2 tbsp extra virgin olive oil
dash of Tabasco or chilli sauce

Thai-style beansprout and shredded vegetable fritters

MAKES 8   PREPARATION **15 MINS**   TO COOK **25 MINS**

If egg rings (or large metal pastry cutters) are not available, mix the vegetables into the batter and drop ladlefuls into the hot oil. Serve two for a light lunch.

INGREDIENTS

½ carrot
60g (2oz) asparagus tips
  (approx. 15cm/6in long)
½ small red pepper, deseeded
  and cut into thin strips
125g (4½oz) plain flour
1 tsp baking powder
¼ tsp ground turmeric
¾ tsp salt
1 tsp grated fresh root ginger
1 tsp finely chopped
  lemongrass or
  lemongrass purée
1 garlic clove, crushed
1 thin red chilli, deseeded
  and finely chopped
4 spring onions, chopped
100g (3½oz) beansprouts
1 tbsp chopped coriander
sunflower oil, for frying
1 tbsp snipped chives, plus
  extra to garnish
noodle and beansprout salad
  and sweet chilli sauce,
  to serve

1 Pare the carrot into thin ribbons with a potato peeler or a mandolin. Cut the asparagus spears in half lengthways and then widthways. Set both aside with the red pepper.

2 Mix the flour with the baking powder, turmeric, salt, ginger, lemongrass, garlic, and chilli. Whisk in 250ml (8fl oz) cold water to form a batter the consistency of thick cream. Stir in the spring onions, beansprouts, and coriander.

3 Place 4 egg rings in a large frying pan. Add about 5mm (¼in) oil and heat until hot, but not smoking.

4 Add about an eighth of the batter (a small ladleful) to one of the egg rings and quickly top with a few strips of each vegetable, pressing gently into the uncooked batter. Repeat with the other rings, using half the ingredients in all. Fry for 2–3 minutes until the batter is puffed up, set, and brown underneath.

5 Lift off the rings with tongs. Flip the fritters over with a fish slice and fry for a further 2 minutes to brown and cook the vegetables. Lift out with a fish slice and drain, vegetable side up, on kitchen paper. Keep warm while cooking the remaining fritters in the same way.

6 Transfer the fritters to serving plates and garnish with a few snipped chives. Serve with a noodle and beansprout salad and some sweet chilli sauce for dipping.

Pan-fries and fritters
Falafel with dill and cucumber dip

SERVES 4   **PREPARATION 20 MINS**   TO COOK **9 MINS**

These falafel balls are particularly appetizing when served with plenty of salad in split, warm pitta breads, with the dip spooned in.

INGREDIENTS

1 onion, roughly chopped
400g can chickpeas, drained
1 small garlic clove, crushed
1 tsp ground cumin
1 tsp ground coriander
2 tbsp roughly
    chopped parsley
salt and freshly ground
    black pepper
½ tsp baking powder
1 egg, separated
splash of milk, if needed
85g (3oz) fresh breadcrumbs
sunflower oil, for frying

For the dip
150g (5½oz) Greek-style
    yogurt
5cm (2in) piece cucumber,
    peeled, deseeded, and grated
1 tsp white balsamic
    condiment
¼ tsp caster sugar
2 tbsp chopped dill

1 To make the falafel, put the onion, chickpeas, garlic, spices, parsley, salt and pepper, and baking powder in a food processor and blend to a thick paste, stopping and scraping down the sides as necessary.

2 Mix in the egg yolk to bind. Add a splash of milk, if necessary, but don't make the mixture too wet.

3 Shape the mixture into 12 small balls and flatten slightly. Coat in lightly beaten egg white, then in the breadcrumbs. Chill, if time allows, until ready to cook.

4 Meanwhile, mix the dip ingredients together and chill until ready to serve.

5 Shallow-fry the falafel in hot oil for about 3 minutes, turning once, until crisp and golden. Drain on kitchen paper. Serve warm or cold with the dip.

Lentil and carrot rissoles

MAKES 8   PREPARATION **20 MINS**   TO COOK **8–12 MINS**

In these tasty rissoles, other roots can be used instead of carrots. **Try a large parsnip to add a sweet earthiness,** or a small celeriac for a subtle celery flavour.

1 Using a food processor or hand blender, purée the lentils to a rough paste.

2 Heat the oil in a saucepan. Add the onion, garlic, and carrots and fry, stirring, for 3 minutes until softened and the onion is lightly golden.

3 Remove from the heat, add the lentils and sage, mix well, and season with salt and pepper.

4 Whisk the egg and yogurt together and add to the mixture to bind. It will be quite wet. Shape the mixture into 8 patties and coat thoroughly in the breadcrumbs, pressing them on firmly as you shape the patties. Place on a plate and chill for at least 30 minutes or overnight, if possible, to firm.

5 Heat about 5mm (¼in) oil in a large frying pan and shallow-fry the patties for 2–3 minutes on each side until crisp and golden, turning once. Cook in two batches.

6 Drain on kitchen paper and serve hot with chutney and a large mixed salad.

INGREDIENTS

2 × 400g cans green lentils, rinsed and drained
1 tbsp sunflower oil, plus extra for frying
1 small onion, finely chopped
1 large garlic clove, crushed
2 large carrots, grated
2 tbsp chopped sage
salt and freshly ground black pepper
1 egg
1 tbsp plain yogurt
100g (3½oz) fresh breadcrumbs
chutney and large mixed salad, to serve

Veggie burgers with melting cheese

MAKES 4   **PREPARATION 15 MINS, PLUS CHILLING**   TO COOK **10 MINS**

It's best to use ready-sliced Gruyère or Emmental cheese for this dish – the slices will **melt perfectly to a lovely gooey finish and add a sweet, nutty tang**.

INGREDIENTS

400g can aduki beans, drained
2 carrots, grated
1 small onion, grated
30g (1oz) chopped mixed nuts
85g (3oz) fresh breadcrumbs
1 tsp dried mixed herbs
1 tbsp mushroom ketchup
  or Worcestershire sauce
salt and freshly ground
  black pepper
1 small egg, beaten
sunflower oil, for frying
4 burger buns, cut in half
tomato ketchup or sweet
  chilli sauce
4 slices Swiss cheese
2 tomatoes, sliced
a little shredded lettuce
chips and coleslaw,
  to serve

1 Mash the beans well in a bowl with a potato masher or fork. Add the carrots, onion, nuts, breadcrumbs, mixed herbs, mushroom ketchup, and some salt and pepper. Combine thoroughly, then mix with just enough of the beaten egg to bind the mixture together.

2 Shape the mixture into 4 burgers, place on baking parchment on a plate, and chill for 30 minutes to firm up.

3 Heat enough oil to cover the base of a large non-stick frying pan. Fry the burgers over a moderate heat for 6–7 minutes on each side until golden brown. Drain on kitchen paper.

4 Preheat the grill. Toast the buns on the cut sides only. Spread with some tomato ketchup. Remove the bun tops from the grill pan, place the burgers on top of the bases, then add a slice of cheese. Flash under the grill until the cheese starts to melt. Top with some sliced tomatoes and a little shredded lettuce.

5 Quickly place the bun tops in place, either completely on top or at a jaunty angle, and serve with chips and coleslaw.

Four ways with
Potatoes

Dauphinoise potatoes ▷

TAKES 2 hrs **SERVES** 4

Preheat the oven to 180°C (350°F/Gas 4). Put 900g (2lb) **waxy potatoes**, peeled and cut into slices 3mm (⅛in) thick, 300ml (10fl oz) **double cream**, and 300ml (10fl oz) **milk** in a large pan. Season with **salt** and freshly ground **black pepper**. Bring to the boil, cover, and simmer for 10–15 minutes, or until the potatoes begin to soften. Using a slotted spoon, transfer the potatoes to a shallow 2.3 litre (4 pint) ovenproof dish. Sprinkle over 3 grated **garlic cloves** and season. Strain the cream and milk mixture, then pour over the potatoes. Cover with foil and bake for 1 hour. Remove the foil and cook for 30 minutes more, or until the top turns golden.

◁ Egg and fennel potato salad

TAKES 25 mins **SERVES** 4

Boil 4 **eggs** for 8 minutes – less if you prefer a runnier yolk. Cook 250g (9oz) **new potatoes** in a large pan of lightly salted boiling water for 15–20 minutes, or until soft. Drain them well and transfer to a serving plate. Drizzle over some **olive oil** while the potatoes are still hot, then season with **salt** and freshly ground **black pepper**. Mix in a handful of finely chopped **flat-leaf parsley** and 1 trimmed and finely chopped **fennel bulb**. Shell and quarter the hard-boiled eggs and add to the potato salad. Serve immediately.

Choose floury potatoes for mash, chips, baking, and roasting, and waxy varieties for gratins, salads, boiling, and steaming. All-purpose potatoes are midway in texture, which makes them extremely versatile.

Cajun-spiced potato wedges ▶

TAKES 45 mins–1 hr **SERVES** 6

Preheat the oven to 200°C (400°F/Gas 6). Cut 4 unpeeled **floury potatoes** into thick wedges. Cook in boiling salted water for 3 minutes; drain. Place in a roasting tin with 1 **lemon**, cut into 6 wedges, 12 **garlic cloves**, 3 **red onions**, cut into 8 wedges, and 4 **bay leaves**. Whisk together 3 tbsp **lemon juice**, 1 tbsp **tomato purée**, **salt** and freshly ground **black pepper**, ½ tsp each **cayenne pepper** and **ground cumin**, 1 tsp each **paprika**, **dried oregano,** and **dried thyme**, and 6 tbsp each **olive oil** and water. Pour evenly over the potatoes and toss. Roast for 30–40 minutes, turning the potatoes frequently. Serve hot.

◀ Potato cakes

TAKES 35 mins **SERVES** 4

Boil 450g (1lb) peeled **floury potatoes** in a pan of salted water for 15–20 minutes until soft. Drain, then mash. Mix the mashed potatoes with 1 peeled and grated **onion**, a handful of fresh **chives**, finely chopped, 125g (4½oz) **feta cheese**, crumbled, and 1 lightly beaten **egg**. Season with **salt** and freshly ground **black pepper**. Heat 1 tbsp **olive oil** in a non-stick frying pan over a medium heat. Using floured hands, scoop up large balls of the potato mixture, roll, and flatten slightly. Carefully add to the hot oil and fry for 2–3 minutes on each side until golden, topping up the pan with more oil, if needed. Serve hot.

Beetroot and caraway blinis with soured cream

SERVES 4–6   **PREPARATION 20 MINS**   TO COOK **40 MINS**

Blinis are usually made with yeast, but **these are just as light and much quicker to make**. They are best eaten fresh, but can be made in advance and reheated.

INGREDIENTS

115g (4oz) plain flour
pinch of salt
2 tsp caster sugar
2 eggs, separated
250ml (9fl oz) milk
1 tbsp caraway seeds
3 large or 6 small cooked
  beetroot, grated
1 large onion, finely chopped
1 tbsp chopped coriander
  or tarragon
200ml (7fl oz) soured cream
  or crème fraîche
sunflower oil, for frying

1 Sift the flour, salt, and sugar into a bowl. Add the egg yolks and half the milk and beat well until smooth.

2 Stir in the remaining milk and add the caraway seeds and a quarter of the beetroot. Whisk the egg whites until stiff and fold in with a metal spoon.

3 Mix the onion with the coriander and place in a small serving dish. Put the remaining beetroot in a second serving dish and the soured cream in a third. Chill until ready to serve.

4 Heat a little oil in a non-stick frying pan. Pour off the excess. Add 3 tbsp batter and spread out to make a pancake about 10cm (4in) in diameter (you may be able to make 2 or 3, depending on the size of the pan). Cook over a medium-high heat for 1–2 minutes or until golden underneath and bubbles have risen and popped to the surface. Flip over and briefly cook the other side. Remove and keep warm while cooking the remainder.

5 Serve the stack of blinis with the beetroot, onion, and coriander mixture and soured cream. To eat, take a blini, add a spoonful of beetroot, then a little onion mixture, and top with a dollop of soured cream. The blinis may also be made much smaller to serve as canapés.

Curries, stews, and casseroles

Kadhai paneer with peppers

SERVES 4–6   PREPARATION **25 MINS**   TO COOK **30 MINS**

A kadhai is an Indian wok, and **this is the Indian answer to a stir-fry**. The sauce can be used with any vegetables and pulses, so make extra and keep it in the fridge.

INGREDIENTS

1 tbsp ghee (clarified butter)
   or sunflower oil
½ tsp crushed dried chillies
2 red peppers, deseeded and
   cut into strips
1 red onion, thickly sliced
500g (1lb 2oz) paneer, cut into
   1cm (½in) batons
1 bunch of coriander, chopped
juice of 1 lemon
5cm (2in) piece fresh root
   ginger, cut into julienne

For the kadhai sauce

3 tbsp ghee or sunflower oil
2 garlic cloves, finely chopped
2 tsp coriander seeds, crushed
2 red chillies, deseeded and
   finely chopped
2 onions, finely chopped
2 tsp grated fresh root ginger
450g (1lb) tomatoes, chopped
1 tbsp crushed dried
   fenugreek leaves
salt
1 tsp sugar (optional)

1 To make the sauce, heat the ghee or oil in a pan, add the garlic, and let it colour but not burn. Stir, then add the coriander seeds and red chillies. When they release their aromas, add the onions and cook until they begin to turn light golden. Stir in the grated ginger and tomatoes. Reduce the heat to low and cook until excess moisture has evaporated and the fat starts to separate, stirring frequently. Add the fenugreek. Taste and add salt and some sugar if needed.

2 For the stir-fry, heat the ghee or oil in a kadhai, wok, or large frying pan. Add the crushed chillies, pepper strips, and red onion. Stir and sauté on a high heat for 2 minutes. Add the paneer and stir for another minute. Now add the sauce and mix well. Once everything is heated through, check for seasoning, adding a touch of salt if required. Finish with the coriander and lemon juice. Garnish with the ginger and serve.

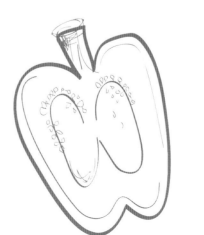

Seasonal vegetables in spinach and garlic sauce

SERVES 4–6 **PREPARATION 25 MINS** TO COOK **20 MINS**

For this dish, **parboil hard vegetables first and add the delicate and green ones later.** Cut all the vegetables to more or less the same shape and size.

1 Parboil the carrots, cauliflower, and green beans until al dente (3 minutes for the cauliflower and green beans, 4 minutes for the carrots). Drain well, refresh in iced water, and drain again.

2 Blanch the spinach in boiling salted water until wilted, then drain and cool quickly in iced water. Squeeze dry. Blend in a food processor to make a smooth paste, adding a little water if required.

3 In a heavy-based pan, heat the ghee or oil over a medium heat. Stir in the cumin seeds for 30 seconds until fragrant, then add the garlic and sauté until golden. Add the onion, reduce the heat to low, and cook, stirring, until soft and golden brown. Stir in the ginger and chillies and sauté for 2–3 minutes.

4 Stir in the carrots and cauliflower and cook for 2–4 minutes before adding the coriander and salt. Then add the mushrooms and sauté, stirring, for 2–3 minutes or until they soften. Add the baby corn and sauté for 1–2 minutes. Next add the beans and peas, mixing together well. Add the chickpea flour and stir for 2–3 minutes, then add the spinach paste and bring to the boil, stirring in the butter and cream.

5 As soon as the vegetables are boiling, check for seasoning and correct if necessary. Finish with the fenugreek leaves and garam masala. Do not cook for too long after adding the spinach paste as it will discolour and make the dish look unappetizing. Serve with rice.

INGREDIENTS

2 young carrots, diced
¼ cauliflower, cut into
   small florets
100g (3½oz) fine green beans,
   cut into short lengths
1kg (2¼lb) baby spinach leaves
5 tbsp ghee or sunflower oil
2 tsp cumin seeds
2 garlic cloves, finely chopped
1 large onion, finely chopped
2.5cm (1in) piece fresh root
   ginger, finely chopped
6 green chillies, deseeded
   and finely chopped
1½ tsp ground coriander
2 tsp salt
100g (3½oz) button
   mushrooms
50g (1¾oz) baby sweetcorn,
   cut into short lengths
60g (2oz) fresh or frozen peas
1 tbsp gram (chickpea) flour
25g (scant 1oz) butter
4 tbsp single cream
1 tsp crushed, dried
   fenugreek leaves
1 tsp garam masala

Mangetout, sweet potato, and cashew nut red curry

SERVES 4   **PREPARATION 10 MINS**   TO COOK **20 MINS**

Cooking the green vegetables quickly retains their colour and texture. Butternut squash or pumpkin can be substituted for sweet potato, and tofu for cashew nuts.

INGREDIENTS

2 tbsp sunflower oil

1 bunch spring onions, cut into short lengths

1 sweet potato (approx. 600g/1lb 5oz), peeled and cut into walnut-sized pieces

1 garlic clove, crushed

1 tsp grated fresh root ginger or galangal

1 tsp finely chopped lemongrass (or lemongrass purée)

3 tbsp Thai red curry paste

400ml can coconut milk

175g (6oz) mangetout, topped and tailed

2 courgettes, cut into batonettes (see p38)

12 cherry tomatoes

115g (4oz) raw cashew nuts

1 tbsp chopped coriander

squeeze of lime juice

jasmine rice, to serve

1 fat red chilli, deseeded and cut into thin strips, to garnish

1 Heat the oil in a large saucepan or wok. Add the spring onions and stir-fry gently for 2 minutes until softened but not coloured. Add the sweet potato and cook, stirring, for 1 minute.

2 Stir in the garlic, ginger, lemongrass, curry paste, and coconut milk. Bring to the boil, reduce the heat, cover, and simmer gently for 10 minutes or until the sweet potato is tender.

3 Meanwhile, cook the mangetout and courgette batonettes in boiling water for 2–3 minutes until just tender. Drain.

4 Stir the mangetout and courgettes into the curry with the tomatoes, nuts, and coriander. Spike with a squeeze of lime juice and simmer for 2 minutes until the tomatoes are softened slightly but still hold their shape. Spoon the curry over jasmine rice served in bowls and garnish with strips of red chilli.

Vegetable dahl with tandoori paneer

SERVES 4   **PREPARATION 20 MINS, PLUS MARINATING**   TO COOK **35 MINS**

Presentation is key to this dish. **Choose the loosest iceberg you can find**, cut off the stump, then carefully peel off four good, bowl-shaped leaves.

INGREDIENTS

900ml (1½ pints)
   vegetable stock
225g (8oz) red lentils
1 tsp ground cumin
1 tsp ground turmeric
½ tsp ground coriander
1 piece of cinnamon stick
2 tbsp sunflower oil
1 onion, chopped
1 garlic clove, crushed
2 tbsp Madras curry paste
2 carrots, diced
2 potatoes, diced
150g (5½oz) green beans,
   cut in short lengths
2 tomatoes, roughly chopped
4 large iceberg lettuce leaves
paprika, to garnish
mango chutney, to serve

For the paneer
250g (9oz) block paneer
2 tbsp tandoori paste
115g (4oz) plain yogurt
1 large garlic clove, crushed
1 tbsp chopped coriander
salt and freshly ground
   black pepper

1 First, prepare the paneer. Cut the block into 4 strips widthways, then cut each strip in half horizontally to make 8 thinner slabs. Make slashes on each side with a sharp knife, just cutting the surface. Mix the tandoori paste with the yogurt, garlic, coriander, and a pinch of salt. Add the paneer, turn to coat completely, then cover and chill for 2 hours.

2 About 40 minutes before you intend to eat, pour the stock into a saucepan. Bring to the boil and add the lentils and spices. Season well. Bring to the boil, reduce the heat, and simmer for 25–30 minutes until the lentils are tender, stirring occasionally. If necessary, boil rapidly for 1–2 minutes to evaporate any remaining liquid.

3 Meanwhile, in a separate pan, heat the oil and fry the onion and garlic for 3 minutes, stirring, until softened and slightly browned. Add the curry paste and fry for 30 seconds, then gently stir in the carrots, potatoes, and beans. Add 150ml (5fl oz) water and salt and pepper. Bring to the boil, reduce the heat, cover, and simmer gently for 10–15 minutes until the vegetables are tender. Remove the lid and boil rapidly to evaporate any remaining liquid, if necessary.

4 Stir the vegetable mixture into the cooked lentils and season to taste. Gently fold in the tomatoes. Cover and keep warm.

5 Oil and preheat a griddle. Shake excess marinade off the paneer. Griddle for 1–2 minutes on each side, pressing down with a fish slice, until striped and brown in places. Remove from the griddle.

6 Spoon the curry into the lettuce on serving plates. Add the paneer. Dust the plates with paprika and serve with mango chutney.

Black-eyed beans with spinach and tomato curry

SERVES 4   PREPARATION **10 MINS**   TO COOK **12 MINS**

A refreshing and light curry, this is **easy to make and very versatile**. Double the quantity of beans for a more substantial meal. Take care not to overcook the yogurt.

INGREDIENTS

3 tbsp sunflower oil
½ tsp mustard seeds
2 garlic cloves, finely chopped
10 curry leaves
1 large onion, chopped
2 green chillies, slit
   lengthways and deseeded
½ tsp chilli powder
1 tsp ground coriander
½ tsp ground turmeric
3 tomatoes, chopped
100g (3½oz) spinach, chopped
400g can black-eyed beans,
   rinsed and drained
salt
300g (10oz) plain yogurt
naan breads, to serve

1 Heat the oil in a large saucepan and add the mustard seeds. When they start to pop, add the garlic, curry leaves, and onion. Cook over a medium heat for 5 minutes, or until the onion is soft.

2 Add the green chillies, chilli powder, coriander, and turmeric. Mix well and add the tomato pieces. Stir, then add the spinach. Cook over a low heat for 5 minutes.

3 Add the black-eyed beans with salt to taste. Cook for another minute, or until everything is hot. Remove the pan from the heat and slowly add the yogurt, stirring well. Serve warm with plenty of naan breads.

Okra and aubergine spicy masala

SERVES 4   **PREPARATION 10 MINS**   TO COOK **20–25 MINS**

Okra and aubergine blend well here with aromatic spices for a fairly mild curry. This can be eaten as a main dish with chapattis or as a fantastic side dish.

1 Heat the oil in a saucepan and add the fenugreek seeds, fennel seeds, cardamom pods, cinnamon stick, bay leaf, garlic, and onions. Cook, stirring occasionally, until the onions are golden brown.

2 Add the turmeric, chilli powder, coriander, and tomato purée and stir well. Cook for another minute. Stir in the tomatoes and 500ml (16fl oz) water. Bring to the boil, then reduce the heat and simmer for about 10 minutes, or until the sauce is thick.

3 Add the okra and aubergine to the sauce with salt to taste and stir thoroughly. Cover and cook on a low heat for 5 minutes, or until the aubergine and okra become tender. Garnish with chopped coriander and serve hot.

INGREDIENTS

3 tbsp sunflower oil
pinch of fenugreek seeds
pinch of fennel seeds
2–3 cardamom pods
2cm (¾in) cinnamon stick
1 bay leaf
3 garlic cloves, chopped
2 onions, finely chopped
½ tsp ground turmeric
½ tsp chilli powder
1 tsp ground coriander
1 tbsp tomato purée
2 tomatoes, finely chopped
150g (5½oz) okra, cut
  into pieces
150g (5½oz) aubergine,
  cut into pieces
salt
2 tbsp chopped coriander
  leaves, to garnish

Quesadilla with avocado, spring onion, and chilli ▶

TAKES 25 mins **MAKES** 1

Put 4 finely chopped **spring onions**, 1–2 **hot red chillies**, deseeded and finely chopped, and juice of ½ **lime** in a bowl. Season with **salt** and freshly ground **black pepper** and mix. Heat 1½ tbsp **olive oil** in a non-stick frying pan, then fry 1 **wheat** or **corn tortilla** for 1 minute. Scatter over ½ sliced **avocado**, leaving some space around the edge. Spoon on the spring onion mixture and sprinkle with 50g (1¾oz) **Cheddar cheese**. Top with another tortilla; press down with the back of a fish slice. Turn the quesadilla over and cook the other side for 1 minute. Slice in half or quarters and serve.

◀ Avocado with roasted cherry tomatoes and paprika dressing

TAKES 20 mins **SERVES** 4

Preheat the oven to 200°C (400°F/Gas 6). Toss 350g (12oz) **cherry tomatoes** with 1 tbsp **olive oil** in a roasting tin. Add some **thyme** leaves and season with **salt** and freshly ground **black pepper**. Roast for 12–15 minutes. Whisk together 90ml (3fl oz) olive oil, 3 tbsp **white wine vinegar**, 1 tsp **paprika**, a pinch of **caster sugar**, and ½ tsp **mayonnaise**. Season. Halve, stone, and peel 2 ripe **avocados**. Slice lengthways without cutting all the way through, then fan out. Place a fan on each plate with some **wild rocket** leaves and the tomatoes. Spoon the dressing over and serve.

The most widely available types of avocado are the dark, knobbly skinned Hass and the green, smooth-skinned Fuerte. Both have a **nutty flavour, creamy-yellow colour, and oily texture**; the latter are easier to peel.

Avocado mousse with lime ▶

TAKES 15 mins, plus chilling **SERVES** 4

Halve and stone 2 large ripe **avocados**. Scoop the flesh into a bowl, add the grated zest and juice of 1 **lime**, and mash until smooth. Beat in 100g (3½oz) **low-fat cream cheese** and season with **salt** and freshly ground **black pepper**. Sprinkle 2 tsp powdered **gelatine** over 2 tbsp water in a small heatproof bowl. Leave for 1 minute, then place the bowl in a pan of hot water and stir the gelatine until it dissolves. Whisk 1 **egg white** in a bowl to form soft peaks. Drizzle the dissolved gelatine into the avocado mixture and stir. Fold in the egg white without knocking out the air. Spoon into ramekins, cover with cling film, and chill for 2 hours.

◀ Avocado, tomato, and mozzarella salad

TAKES 20 mins **SERVES** 4

Preheat the grill to the highest setting. Put 200g (7oz) small **plum tomatoes** on a baking tray. Add **salt** and freshly gound **black pepper**, 2 sliced **garlic cloves**, and 2 chopped **spring onions**. Drizzle with 4 tbsp **extra virgin olive oil**. Grill for 4–5 minutes. Place in a bowl with the juices. Add 2 tbsp **balsamic vinegar**, 2 tbsp **capers**, rinsed, 150g (5½oz) torn **buffalo mozzarella**, and shredded **basil leaves**. Toss gently. Peel, stone, and quarter 2 ripe **avocados**. Place 2 quarters on each plate. Spoon the tomato mixture over and drizzle with balsamic vinegar. Serve immediately.

Red bean and chestnut bourguignon

SERVES 4–6   **PREPARATION 25 MINS**   TO COOK **1¼–1½ HRS**

The chestnuts add a wonderful texture to this rich and flavoursome casserole – elegant enough for a dinner party, but good with homely jacket potatoes too.

INGREDIENTS

1 tbsp olive oil
30g (1oz) butter
2 red onions, quartered
1 garlic clove, crushed
16 baby Chantenay carrots
  (approx. 115g/4oz),
  topped and tailed
8 baby turnips, peeled but
  left whole, or 2 larger ones,
  cut into chunks
150g (5½oz) crimini or white
  button mushrooms
2 tbsp plain flour
300ml (10fl oz) red wine
300ml (10fl oz) vegetable stock
2 tbsp brandy
1 tbsp tomato purée
good pinch of caster sugar
240g can cooked,
  peeled chestnuts
400g can red kidney beans,
  rinsed and drained
1 bouquet garni sachet
salt and freshly ground
  black pepper
fluffy mash or jacket potatoes
  and broccoli, to serve

1 Preheat the oven to 180°C (350°F/Gas 4). Heat the oil and butter in a flameproof casserole and fry the onions for 5 minutes, stirring, until richly browned.

2 Add the garlic, carrots, turnips, and mushrooms and fry for 2 minutes. Stir in the flour and cook for 1 minute. Gradually blend in the wine, stock, brandy, and tomato purée. Bring to the boil, stirring, until slightly thickened.

3 Stir in the sugar, chestnuts, beans, bouquet garni, and salt and pepper to taste. Cover the surface with wet baking parchment, then add the lid and cook in the oven for 1¼–1½ hours until the vegetables are really tender. Discard the bouquet garni, stir gently, then taste and adjust the seasoning if necessary. Serve hot with fluffy mash or jacket potatoes and broccoli.

Creamy mixed bean ragout with shredded kale

SERVES 4   PREPARATION **15 MINS**   TO COOK **25 MINS**

The slightly bitter flavour of kale blends beautifully with the earthy beans and the sweet taste of celeriac. Try different roots such as parsnips, carrots, or turnips too.

INGREDIENTS

2 tbsp olive oil

1 leek, sliced

2 garlic cloves, chopped

1 tsp ground cumin

1 tsp crushed dried chillies

½ tsp ground turmeric

2 star anise

750ml (1¼ pints)
   vegetable stock

2 × 400g cans mixed
   pulses, drained

1 small celeriac, diced

115g (4oz) button mushrooms

1 bay leaf

salt and freshly ground
   black pepper

250g (9oz) kale, finely
   shredded, discarding
   thick stumps

handful of coriander, chopped

2 tbsp tahini paste

200g (7oz) crème fraîche

dash of lemon juice

1 Heat the oil in a large saucepan. Add the leek and fry, stirring, for 1 minute. Add the garlic and spices and fry for 30 seconds. Stir in the stock, mixed pulses, celeriac, and mushrooms. Add the bay leaf, a little salt, and a generous grinding of pepper. Bring to the boil, reduce the heat, partially cover, and simmer gently for 15 minutes.

2 Add the kale, stir, and bring back to the boil. Reduce the heat, cover, and simmer for a further 8 minutes until everything is really tender. Discard the bay leaf and star anise.

3 Gently stir in the coriander, tahini paste, and all but 2 tsp of the crème fraîche. Add lemon juice to taste and adjust the seasoning, if necessary.

4 Ladle into warmed bowls and add a swirl of the reserved crème fraîche.

Sweet potato, roasted pepper, and white bean hotpot

SERVES 4   **PREPARATION 20 MINS**   TO COOK **1 HR 10 MINS**

In this simple casserole, the **sweet potatoes are cooked on top for added texture and flavour**. They can be diced and added to the mixture before cooking, if preferred.

1 Preheat the oven to 190°C (375°F/Gas 5). Heat the oil in a flameproof casserole and fry the onion for 3 minutes, stirring, until softened, but not browned. Add the garlic and carrots and fry for 1 minute.

2 Add the wine, bring to a rapid boil and cook for about 2 minutes until the wine is well reduced.

3 Add the remaining ingredients except the sweet potatoes and butter. Stir well and season with salt and pepper. Bring to the boil.

4 Layer the sweet potatoes on top and brush liberally with the butter. Cover with the lid or foil and bake in the oven for 30 minutes. Increase the temperature to 220°C (425°F/Gas 7) and cook for a further 20–30 minutes until the potatoes are golden and tender. Serve hot with broccoli and jacket potatoes.

INGREDIENTS

2 tbsp olive oil
1 large onion, chopped
2 garlic cloves, crushed
2 carrots, sliced
150ml (5fl oz) dry white wine
2 red peppers, roasted (see p44) and chopped
115g (4oz) closed-cup mushrooms, quartered
2 × 400g cans haricot beans, drained
400g can chopped tomatoes
120ml (4fl oz) vegetable stock
2 tbsp oat bran
1 tbsp chopped thyme
generous pinch of caster sugar
salt and freshly ground black pepper
2 sweet potatoes, cut into 5mm (¼in) slices
20g (¾oz) butter, melted
broccoli and jacket potatoes, to serve

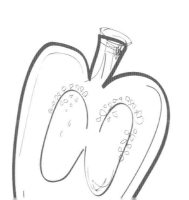

Pizzas, wraps, and quesadillas

Cheese, tomato, and mushroom pizza

MAKES 2 LARGE OR 4 SMALL PIZZAS   PREPARATION **20 MINS, PLUS PROVING**   TO COOK **35 MINS**

This pizza is delicious with the addition of a **handful of rocket on top to add a cool, peppery finish** to each bite. For a classic Margherita pizza, omit the mushrooms.

INGREDIENTS

450g (1lb) strong plain flour, plus extra for dusting
1 tsp salt
1 tsp caster sugar
2 tsp fast-action dried yeast
2 tbsp olive oil, plus extra for greasing and drizzling

For the topping

2 tbsp olive oil
1 small onion, finely chopped
2 garlic cloves, crushed
400g can chopped tomatoes
1 tbsp tomato purée
2 tsp dried oregano
pinch of sugar
salt and freshly ground black pepper
115g (4oz) crimini mushrooms, sliced
300g (10oz) mozzarella cheese, drained and torn into pieces
large handful of black olives
a few basil leaves

1 Mix the flour, salt, sugar, and yeast together in a large bowl. Gradually add 300ml (10fl oz) warm water and 2 tbsp oil and stir until combined. Mix with your hands to bring it into a ball, then tip out onto a lightly floured surface and knead for at least 5 minutes, adding a little more flour if needed, until the dough is springy to the touch, but not sticky. Shape into a ball and place in a large lightly oiled bowl. Cover with lightly oiled cling film and leave to prove for 1 hour in a warm place, or until it has doubled in size.

2 Meanwhile, make the topping. Heat the oil in a saucepan, then add the onion and sauté over a medium heat for 5 minutes. Stir in the garlic and cook for 1 minute. Add the tomatoes, tomato purée, oregano, and sugar. Season with salt and pepper and simmer uncovered for 10 minutes until pulpy. Set aside.

3 Preheat the oven to 220°C (425°F/Gas 7). Knead the risen dough again, then roll out to two 30–35cm (12–14in) rounds or 4 smaller rounds (about 20cm/8in). Place on oiled pizza plates or baking sheets and press out the rounds again with floured fingers. Alternatively, roll out to 2 large rectangles that just fit the baking sheets and press them into shape once transferred.

4 Divide the tomato sauce, sliced mushrooms, mozzarella, and olives between the pizzas. Season with pepper and drizzle with a little oil. Bake each pizza for 18–20 minutes until crisp and golden around the edges. Scatter with a few basil leaves before serving.

Spinach, fresh tomato, and blue cheese pizza

MAKES 2 LARGE OR 4 SMALL PIZZAS   PREPARATION **20 MINS, PLUS PROVING**   TO COOK **20 MINS**

Try topping each pizza with six quail's eggs 5 minutes before the end of the cooking time, making tiny wells in the surface of the pizza first.

1 Make and prove the pizza dough (see p120, step 1). While the dough is proving, put the tomatoes in a bowl and cover with boiling water. Leave for 30 seconds, drain, plunge in cold water, then remove the skins and chop the flesh. Mix with the tomato purée, sugar, and some salt and pepper.

2 Shake the excess water from the spinach. Cook the spinach in a pan with no extra water for about 3 minutes until wilted, stirring. Drain thoroughly. Leave to cool, then squeeze out the excess liquid.

3 Preheat the oven to 220°C (425°F/Gas 7). Knead the risen dough again, then roll out to two 30–35cm (12–14in) rounds or 4 smaller rounds (about 20cm/8in). Place on oiled pizza plates or baking sheets and press out the rounds again with floured fingers. Alternatively, roll out to 2 large rectangles that just fit the baking sheets and press them into shape once transferred.

4 Spread the tomato mixture over the dough, not quite to the edges. Scatter the spinach and cheeses over. Sprinkle with the chopped sage, drizzle with a little more oil, and season with pepper. Bake each pizza for 18–20 minutes until crisp and golden around the edges.

INGREDIENTS

1 quantity pizza dough
 (see p120)
8 ripe tomatoes
6 tbsp tomato purée
1 tsp caster sugar
salt and freshly ground
 black pepper
450g (1lb) spinach,
 well washed
200g (7oz) blue cheese,
 crumbled
200g (7oz) mozzarella
 cheese, grated
12 sage leaves, chopped

Beetroot, courgette, and goat's cheese pizzas

MAKES 2 LARGE OR 4 SMALL PIZZAS   **PREPARATION 30 MINS, PLUS PROVING**   TO COOK **20 MINS**

When time is short, use two 290g (10oz) pizza base mixes. **Try this with peppers instead of courgettes** and slices of baby Camembert for a variation on goat's cheese.

INGREDIENTS

1 quantity pizza dough
  (see p120)
5 tbsp olive oil
4 small courgettes, sliced
1 red onion, halved and
  thinly sliced
1 large garlic clove,
  finely chopped
2 tbsp chopped rosemary
150ml (5fl oz) passata
2 tbsp tomato purée
2 cooked beetroots (in
  natural juices), diced
4 handfuls of wild rocket,
  plus extra to garnish
2 × 120g cylinders goat's
  cheese, sliced
coarse sea salt
freshly ground black pepper

1 Make and prove the pizza dough (see p120, step 1). While it is proving, heat 3 tbsp oil in a frying pan. Add the courgettes, onion, garlic, and rosemary and cook, stirring, for 3 minutes until softened, but not browned. Set aside.

2 When the dough has proved, preheat the oven to 220°C (425°F/ Gas 7). Knead the risen dough. Roll out to two 30–35cm (12–14in) rounds or four 20cm (8in) rounds and place on oiled pizza plates or baking sheets. Press out the rounds again with floured fingers, then place in the oven and bake for 10 minutes to cook them partially.

3 Mix the passata with the tomato purée. Remove the pizzas from the oven and spread the tomato mixture over, followed by the courgette and onion mixture. Scatter with the beetroot and rocket, then arrange the goat's cheese slices on top. Sprinkle with a little salt and add a good grinding of pepper to each.

4 Bake in the oven for a further 10 minutes until the crust is golden brown, the cheese is melting, and everything is hot through.

5 Top with a little rocket and drizzle each pizza with the remaining oil before serving.

Vegetable-stuffed pizzas

MAKES 4 **PREPARATION 25 MINS, PLUS PROVING** TO COOK **20 MINS**

Vary the vegetables according to what you have on hand – cooked carrots, potatoes, or shredded greens could be added, or use peas instead of sweetcorn.

INGREDIENTS

1 quantity pizza dough
  (see p120)
4 tbsp tomato purée
250g (9oz) mozzarella cheese,
  torn into pieces
4 tbsp grated
  Parmesan cheese
4 small tomatoes, chopped
4 white cup or chestnut
  mushrooms, chopped
200g can sweetcorn, drained
1 tbsp capers (optional)
4 generous pinches
  of dried basil
1 tsp smoked paprika
salt and freshly ground
  black pepper
2 tbsp olive oil, plus extra
  for greasing
150ml (5fl oz) passata, to serve

1 Make and prove the dough (see p120, step 1). Preheat the oven to 220°C (425°F/Gas 7). Cut the dough evenly into 4 and shape into balls. Roll out each ball into a circle about 20cm (8in) in diameter. Spread a little tomato purée on each circle, leaving a 3cm (1¼in) border all around. Divide the mozzarella cheese between the circles and sprinkle each with ½ tbsp Parmesan cheese.

2 Top with the tomatoes, mushrooms, sweetcorn, capers (if using), and basil. Season with paprika and salt and pepper, then drizzle with half the oil.

3 Brush the edges with water, draw the dough up over the filling, and press the edges together to seal. Invert on an oiled baking sheet. Brush with the remaining oil and bake in the oven for about 20 minutes until crisp and golden.

4 Meanwhile, heat the passata in a saucepan. Place the stuffed pizzas on warmed plates. Spoon the passata over and sprinkle with the remaining grated Parmesan.

Purple sprouting broccoli, ricotta, and rosemary calzones

MAKES 4   **PREPARATION 30 MINS, PLUS PROVING**   TO COOK **25 MINS**

A calzone is the pizza equivalent of a pasty. The dough is folded over the filling and the edge sealed before baking so **all the flavour is encased in the dough**.

1 Make and prove the dough (see p120, step 1). Preheat the oven to 220°C (425°F/Gas 7). Steam or boil the broccoli for 3–4 minutes until it is just tender. Drain, rinse with cold water, and drain again. Chop into bite-sized pieces and set aside.

2 Cut the dough into 4 equal pieces and roll out to 20cm (8in) rounds on a lightly floured surface. Mash the butter, garlic, rosemary, ricotta, and salt and pepper together and spread over the rounds of dough, leaving a 3cm (1¼in) border all around.

3 Add the chopped broccoli, tomatoes, mozzarella, and olives, leaving the border clear. Drizzle with half the oil.

4 Brush the edges with water. Using lightly floured hands, fold the calzones in half and press the edges together, then roll over the edge to seal. Transfer to an oiled baking sheet and brush the tops with oil. Bake in the oven for 18–20 minutes, or until crisp and golden. Garnish with a dusting of grated Parmesan cheese.

INGREDIENTS

1 quantity pizza dough (see p120)
200g (7oz) purple sprouting broccoli, thick stalks removed
flour, for dusting
60g (2oz) butter, softened
2 large garlic cloves, crushed
2 tbsp chopped rosemary
150g (5½oz) ricotta cheese
salt and freshly ground black pepper
2 large tomatoes, chopped
85g (3oz) mozzarella cheese, torn into pieces
4 tbsp sliced black olives
2 tbsp olive oil, plus extra for greasing
2 tbsp grated Parmesan cheese, to garnish

Griddled asparagus, mushroom, and garlic sauce pizzas

MAKES 2 LARGE OR 4 SMALL PIZZAS   **PREPARATION 30 MINS, PLUS PROVING**   TO COOK **30 MINS**

When asparagus isn't in season, **try this pizza with strips of aubergine sliced lengthways and griddled.** Fresh, green garlic works particularly well here too.

INGREDIENTS

1 quantity pizza dough
   (see p120)
150g (5½oz) thin asparagus
   spears, trimmed
5–6 tbsp olive oil
2 shallots, chopped
250g (9oz) mixed speciality
   mushrooms such as
   shiitake, enoki, and
   nomeku, sliced if large
4 leaves spring greens or
   other green cabbage,
   (approx. 100g/3½oz),
   finely shredded, discarding
   any thick stalks
30g (1oz) butter
3 tbsp plain flour
250ml (9fl oz) milk
2 large garlic cloves, crushed
85g (3oz) Cheddar
   cheese, grated
salt and freshly ground
   black pepper
2 tbsp chopped tarragon
   or basil
125g (4½oz) mozzarella
   cheese, grated
2 tbsp snipped chives

1 Make and prove the pizza dough (see p120, step 1). While the dough is proving, preheat a griddle. Brush the asparagus spears with a little oil and cook on a griddle for 2 minutes on each side, until bright green with brown stripes and just tender. Cut in diagonal short lengths. Set aside.

2 Heat 2 tbsp oil and sauté the shallots and mushrooms for 2 minutes until softened. Remove from the pan and set aside. Add a further 1 tbsp oil to the pan and stir-fry the greens for 2 minutes, stirring until slightly softened. Set aside.

3 When the dough has proved, preheat the oven to 220°C (425°F/ Gas 7). Knead the risen dough. Roll out to two 30–35cm (12–14in) rounds or four 20cm (8in) rounds and place on oiled pizza plates or baking sheets. Press out the rounds again with floured fingers, then place in the oven and bake for 10 minutes to cook them partially.

4 Meanwhile, melt the butter in a small saucepan. Work in the flour with a wire whisk and cook, stirring, for 1 minute. Remove the pan from the heat and whisk in the milk. Return to the heat, bring to the boil, and cook for 2 minutes, whisking constantly until thickened. Stir in the garlic, Cheddar cheese, and salt and pepper to taste.

5 Spread the garlic sauce over the pizzas. Top with the greens, mushrooms, and asparagus. Sprinkle with the tarragon or basil, then the mozzarella. Drizzle with a little oil and sprinkle with the chives. Bake for 15–20 minutes until the pizzas are golden around the edges and crisp. Serve hot, cut into wedges.

Avocado, baby spinach, and chilli wraps

MAKES 2 **PREPARATION** **5 MINS**

Packed with flavour and nutrients, **these wraps make a tasty lunch or snack supper.** Peppery wild rocket or watercress make delicious alternatives to baby spinach.

INGREDIENTS

1 small avocado
1 tsp lemon or lime juice
1 large flour tortilla
2 tbsp mayonnaise
large handful of
    baby spinach
½ red pepper, deseeded
    and cut into thin strips
½ tsp crushed dried chillies
6 slices pickled jalapeño
    chilli pepper
freshly ground black pepper

1 Peel and halve the avocado and remove the stone (see pp42–3). Slice thinly and toss in the lemon or lime juice.

2 Put the tortilla on a board. Spread with the mayonnaise, then add the spinach, avocado, red pepper, chillies, and jalapeño chilli pepper, one after the other. Season with plenty of pepper. Fold in the sides and roll up firmly, then cut in half and serve.

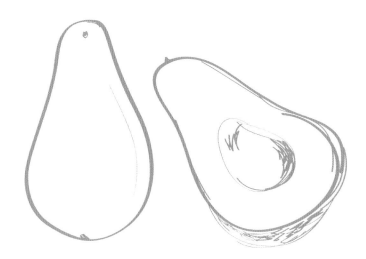

Chilli bean fajitas

MAKES 8   PREPARATION **20 MINS**   TO COOK **20 MINS**

Fajitas are perfect for a colourful, informal meal. To turn them into enchiladas, smother with grated cheese in an ovenproof dish and bake in a hot oven until melted.

1 Heat the oil in a large frying pan or wok. Add all the vegetables, cover, and cook for 5–10 minutes until fairly soft, stirring occasionally.

2 Add the garlic and spices and fry for 30 seconds, then stir in the oregano, tomatoes, and tomato purée. Cover and cook, stirring occasionally, for a further 5 minutes until just tender. Add salt and pepper to taste.

3 Put the refried beans in a separate pan and heat through, stirring. Warm the tortillas briefly in the microwave, if liked.

4 Taking each tortilla in turn, spread with a little of the refried beans, then some of the vegetable mixture. Top with 1 tbsp crème fraîche and a little cheese and roll up. Serve immediately with a crisp green salad.

INGREDIENTS

2 tbsp olive oil
1 large onion, halved
    and sliced
2 red peppers, halved,
    deseeded, and sliced
2 green peppers, halved,
    deseeded, and sliced
2 courgettes, sliced
150g (5½oz) green
    cabbage, shredded
1 large garlic clove, crushed
2 tsp ground cumin
1 tsp crushed dried chillies
1 tsp dried oregano
4 tomatoes, chopped
2 tbsp tomato purée
salt and freshly ground
    black pepper
435g can refried beans
8 flour or corn tortillas
8 tbsp crème fraîche
115g (4oz) Cheddar
    cheese, grated
crisp green salad, to serve

Guacamole and Cheddar quesadillas

MAKES 2   PREPARATION **5 MINS**   TO COOK **5 MINS**

The Mexican tomato, onion, and coriander salsa on pp184-5 is excellent with these quesadillas. **Make sure the avocados are ripe** or they may taste bitter.

INGREDIENTS

2 avocados
2 tsp lime juice
1 tsp crushed dried
  chillies, or to taste
2 thin spring onions,
  finely chopped
5cm (2in) piece cucumber,
  finely chopped
2 tomatoes, deseeded and
  finely chopped
salt and freshly ground
  black pepper
4 flour tortillas
2 large handfuls of grated
  Cheddar cheese
2 tbsp chopped coriander
a few drops of Worcestershire
  sauce or mushroom ketchup

1 For the guacamole, halve, stone, and peel the avocados (see pp42–3). Put the flesh in a bowl and mash well with the lime juice, then mix in the chillies, spring onions, cucumber, and tomatoes. Add salt and pepper to taste.

2 Heat a large non-stick frying pan. Put one tortilla on a board and spread with half the guacamole. Place in the frying pan and scatter over half the cheese and then half the coriander. Add a few drops of Worcestershire sauce and top with a second tortilla. Press down well with a fish slice.

3 Cook for 2–3 minutes over a medium heat until the base is crisp and brown and the cheese is beginning to melt, pressing down constantly. Invert the tortilla onto a plate, then slide back into the pan and cook the other side for about 2 minutes, pressing down again, until the cheese has melted and the base is crisp and brown. Tip out onto a plate and cut into quarters. Keep warm while making the second quesadilla in the same way.

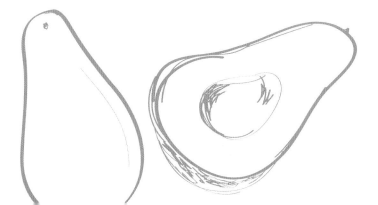

Four ways with
Tomatoes

Tomato soup ▷

TAKES 1 hr 15 mins **SERVES** 4

Heat 1 tbsp **olive oil** in a large saucepan over a medium-low heat. Add 1 chopped **onion**, 1 sliced **garlic clove**, and 2 sliced **celery** sticks, then fry, stirring, until soft, but not coloured. Add 1 sliced **carrot**, 1 chopped **potato**, and stir for 1 minute. Add two 400g cans **chopped tomatoes** with their juice, 750ml (1¼ pints) **vegetable stock**, 1 **bay leaf**, and 1 tsp **sugar**. Add **salt** and freshly ground **black pepper**, bring to the boil, reduce the heat, cover, and simmer for 45 minutes. Remove from the heat and allow to cool slightly, then process in a blender or food processor until smooth. Taste and adjust the seasoning, then reheat and serve.

◁ Baked stuffed tomatoes

TAKES 1 hr, plus standing **SERVES** 4

Cut 4 large ripe **beef tomatoes** in half horizontally. Scoop out the insides and discard. Sprinkle the tomatoes with **salt** and drain upside down for 30 minutes. Preheat the oven to 220°C (425°F/Gas 7). Heat 1 tbsp **olive oil** in a pan, then add 2 finely chopped **anchovies** and 1 crushed **garlic clove**. Cook for 30 seconds. Stir in 4 tbsp fresh **breadcrumbs** and cook for 2 minutes. Mix 4 tbsp **mascarpone** cheese, 125g (4½oz) **ricotta** cheese, and 2 tbsp finely chopped **basil leaves**. Season with freshly ground **black pepper**. Fill each tomato with the cheeses and top with the breadcrumb mixture. Bake for 15–20 minutes.

For salads, choose classic globe tomatoes, cherry tomatoes, or the Brandywine beef variety (for slicing). For sauces, soups, grilling, and roasting, **plum and beef tomatoes have the best flavour**.

Tomato, red onion, and mozzarella salad ▶

TAKES 10 mins **SERVES** 4

Put 8 ripe **plum tomatoes**, sliced, 6 **cherry tomatoes**, halved, 1 small **red onion**, peeled and sliced, and a small handful of torn **basil leaves** in a large bowl. Drizzle over plenty of **extra virgin olive oil**, season well with **salt** and freshly ground **black pepper**, and toss. Arrange 2 handfuls of **wild rocket leaves** on a plate, drizzle over a little oil and some **balsamic vinegar**, and season. Spoon over the tomato and basil mixture. Add 2 balls of **mozzarella**, torn. Scatter some basil leaves over and drizzle with a little oil and balsamic vinegar. Serve immediately.

◀ Chunky tomato sauce

TAKES 35 mins **MAKES** 600ml (1 pint)

Heat 4 tbsp **sunflower oil** in a large saucepan over a medium heat. Add 1 chopped **onion** and 1 chopped **garlic clove**. Fry, stirring occasionally, for 5–8 minutes, or until soft and golden. Stir in 4 tbsp **tomato purée**, two 400g cans **chopped tomatoes** with their juice, 4 torn **basil leaves**, and **salt** and freshly ground **black pepper** to taste. Lower the heat and simmer, uncovered, for 20 minutes, or until the sauce has thickened. Stir in a few more torn basil leaves just before serving.

Tortillas, frittatas, and omelettes

Sweet potato and leek tortilla with fresh tomato sauce

SERVES 4   PREPARATION **15 MINS**   TO COOK **15 MINS**

Tortillas always contain potato, which differentiates them from frittatas. These **use sweet potatoes, as they go so well with leeks**, but ordinary potatoes can be substituted.

INGREDIENTS

1 small sweet potato
   (approx. 450g/1lb),
   peeled, halved
   lengthways, and thinly
   sliced crossways
30g (1oz) butter
2 tbsp olive oil
2 leeks, thinly sliced
2 tbsp chopped thyme,
   plus extra to garnish
6 large eggs, beaten

For the tomato sauce
1 tbsp olive oil
1 garlic clove, crushed
2 beef tomatoes,
   skinned and chopped
1 tbsp tomato purée
generous pinch of
   caster sugar
½ tsp ground cinnamon
salt and freshly ground
   black pepper

1 First, make the tomato sauce. Heat the oil in a saucepan, add the garlic and tomatoes, and fry, stirring, for 2 minutes until the juices are running. Stir in the tomato purée, sugar, cinnamon, and a little salt and pepper. Cover and simmer gently for 5 minutes. Remove the lid and boil rapidly for about 3 minutes until thick and pulpy, stirring constantly. Remove from the heat, then reheat when ready to serve.

2 Bring a pan of water to the boil, drop in the slices of sweet potato, and cook for 4–5 minutes until they are just tender but still holding their shape. Drain thoroughly.

3 Heat the butter and oil in a large non-stick frying pan. Add the leeks and fry over a medium heat for 2 minutes. Add the sweet potatoes, thyme, and salt and pepper. Toss gently until thoroughly combined. Add the beaten eggs and cook gently for 4–5 minutes, lifting and stirring at first, until the egg has almost set.

4 Meanwhile, preheat the grill. Put the frying pan under the grill for a few minutes to brown and set the top of the tortilla. Slide out onto a plate and garnish with a few thyme leaves. Cut into wedges and serve with the tomato sauce.

Courgettes stuffed with sultanas, red onion, and pine nuts ▶

TAKES 30 mins **SERVES** 4

Preheat the oven to 200°C (400°F/Gas 6). Halve 8 **courgettes** lengthways. Scoop out the flesh, chop, and set aside. Heat 1 tbsp **olive oil** in a frying pan over a low heat. Add 1 finely chopped **red onion** and a pinch of **salt**. Sweat for 5 minutes until soft, then stir in the courgette flesh and a pinch of **chilli flakes**. Cook for 2 more minutes. Stir in a small handful each of toasted **pine nuts** and **sultanas**. Remove from the heat. Spoon the mixture into the shells. Top with 75g (2½oz) crumbled **feta cheese**. Roast in the oven for 10–15 minutes. Drizzle with olive oil and serve.

◀ Moroccan couscous salad

TAKES 10 mins **SERVES** 4

Put 250g (9oz) **couscous** in a large bowl with just enough hot **vegetable stock** to cover. Seal with cling film and leave for 5 minutes, then fluff up with a fork. Chop 2 **courgettes**. Heat a little **olive oil** in a frying pan and cook the courgettes until golden. Add to the couscous with a good pinch of **paprika**, the juice of 2 **lemons**, and a handful each of finely chopped fresh **flat-leaf parsley** and chopped **olives**. Season well with **salt** and freshly ground **black pepper** and stir to combine.

Courgettes cook quickly and **can be steamed, boiled, sautéed, or baked**. Just top and tail, then slice, cut in batons, or chop. Cook baby ones whole, or stuff larger ones. **The flowers are also delicious stuffed and fried.**

Grated courgettes with goat's cheese omelette ▶

TAKES 15 mins **SERVES** 1

Put 3 lightly beaten **eggs** and 1 small grated **courgette** in a jug. Season with **sea salt** and freshly ground **black pepper**. Melt a knob of **butter** in a non-stick frying pan over a medium-high heat until foaming, then pour in the egg mixture, swirling it around to cover the base. When it begins to cook around the edges, scatter over 50g (1¾oz) crumbled **soft goat's cheese** evenly. Cook until the centre is almost cooked, but still a little wet. Remove from the heat and leave for 2 minutes to set. Sprinkle a little pepper over, carefully slide out of the pan, and serve.

◀ Courgette fritters with dill tzatziki

TAKES 30 mins, plus draining **SERVES** 4

Grate 200g (7oz) **courgettes**, sprinkle with 1 tsp **salt**, and drain in a sieve for 1 hour. Rinse and squeeze dry. Whisk together 100g (3½oz) **ricotta cheese**, 1 **egg**, and 2 tbsp **plain flour**. Add 2 crushed **garlic cloves** and a small handful each of chopped **basil** and **flat-leaf parsley**. Season well with **salt** and freshly ground **black pepper**. Mix in the courgettes. Fry tablespoons of the batter in **olive oil** for 2–3 minutes on each side. Drain. Serve with tzatziki made with 1 crushed **garlic clove**, 2 tbsp chopped **dill**, 200g (7oz) **Greek-style yogurt**, a squeeze of **lemon juice**, and salt and pepper.

Butternut squash, spinach, and goat's cheese frittata

SERVES 4   **PREPARATION 10 MINS**   TO COOK **20 MINS**

This fresh-tasting frittata is equally good with chopped Swiss chard or pak choi instead of the spinach. Use cottage cheese instead of soft goat's cheese, if preferred.

INGREDIENTS

1 small butternut squash
   (approx. 500g/1lb 2oz),
   peeled, halved, deseeded,
   and diced
2 tbsp olive oil
knob of butter
1 small onion, chopped
200g (7oz) spinach
125g (4½oz) soft
   goat's cheese
4 pieces of semi-dried
   tomatoes in oil, drained
   and cut into small pieces
2 tbsp grated
   Parmesan cheese
grated nutmeg
2 tbsp chopped tarragon
6 eggs, beaten
salt and freshly ground
   black pepper

1 Blanch the squash in boiling water for 2–4 minutes to soften slightly. Drain thoroughly.

2 Heat the oil and butter in a large non-stick frying pan. Add the onion and fry, stirring, for 3 minutes until softened and lightly golden. Add the squash and fry, stirring, for 2 minutes until tender, but still holding its shape.

3 Scatter the spinach into the pan and cook, stirring, for 2 minutes to wilt. Boil rapidly for 1–2 minutes to drive off any liquid, stirring gently and spreading the spinach evenly into the squash. Add small spoonfuls or pieces of the goat's cheese and semi-dried tomatoes. Sprinkle with Parmesan, dust with nutmeg, and scatter the tarragon over.

4 Season the beaten eggs with a little salt and plenty of pepper. Pour into the pan and cook, lifting and stirring, until beginning to set. Cover the pan and cook gently for about 5 minutes until the eggs are almost set and the base is golden.

5 Meanwhile, preheat the grill. When the eggs are nearly set, put the pan under the grill for about 3 minutes to finish setting – the frittata should only just be starting to brown so that all the colours remain vibrant. Remove from the grill and leave to cool for at least 5 minutes. Serve warm or cold, cut into wedges.

Cheese soufflé omelette with sweetcorn and pepper

MAKES 1   PREPARATION **15 MINS**   TO COOK **6 MINS**

If making more than one omelette, **serve each as it is ready** as their lovely texture is rapidly lost as they cool. Serve with crusty bread and a green salad.

INGREDIENTS

2 eggs, separated
knob of butter

For the sauce
knob of butter
handful of fresh or thawed
   frozen sweetcorn kernels
½ small red pepper, deseeded
   and finely chopped
2 tsp cornflour
7 tbsp milk
2 tsp snipped chives,
   plus a few extra
   to garnish
20g (¾oz) Gruyère
   cheese, grated
20g (¾oz) Cheddar
   cheese, grated
pinch of cayenne pepper
salt and freshly ground
   black pepper

1 To make the sauce, heat the butter in a saucepan. Add the corn and red pepper, stir, then cover and cook very gently for 5 minutes or until tender. Stir in the cornflour, followed by the milk. Bring to the boil and cook for 2 minutes, stirring all the time, until thick. Stir in the chives, cheeses, cayenne, and salt and pepper to taste.

2 Beat the egg yolks with 2 tbsp water and add salt and pepper. Whisk the egg whites until stiff and fold into the yolks with a metal spoon.

3 Preheat the grill. Heat a knob of butter in an omelette pan, add the egg mixture, and gently spread it out. Cook over a medium heat for about 3 minutes until golden underneath. Immediately place the pan under the grill and cook for 2–3 minutes until risen and golden on top. Meanwhile, reheat the sauce, stirring.

4 Slide the omelette out onto a plate. Quickly spread one half with the cheese and corn sauce (don't worry if it oozes over the edge). Flip the uncovered side over the top to fold the omelette in half, and garnish with a few snipped chives. Serve immediately.

Tarts, pies, and parcels

Stuffed portobello mushroom en croûte

SERVES 4   PREPARATION **30 MINS**   TO COOK **45 MINS**

Chestnuts make a hearty, flavoursome filling for mushrooms. These pies are delicious served with new potatoes and a selection of baby vegetables.

INGREDIENTS

1 tbsp olive oil
knob of butter
1 onion, finely chopped
1 celery stick, finely chopped
240g can cooked chestnuts
2 tbsp chopped
   flat-leaf parsley
2 tbsp chopped thyme
1 tsp grated lemon zest
2 tbsp mushroom ketchup
   or Worcestershire sauce
60g (2oz) wholemeal
   breadcrumbs
salt and freshly ground
   black pepper
2 small eggs
4 large portobello mushrooms,
   peeled and stalks reserved
450g packet puff pastry
sprigs of parsley, to garnish

For the sauce

2 tbsp sunflower oil
175g (6oz) chestnut
   mushrooms, finely chopped
1 garlic clove, crushed
150ml (5fl oz) dry cider
200ml (7fl oz) double cream
2 tsp chopped thyme

1 Heat the oil and butter in a saucepan. Add the onion and celery and fry, stirring, for 3 minutes until softened and lightly golden. Remove from the heat, add the chestnuts, and mash with a fork. Work in the herbs, lemon zest, ketchup, breadcrumbs, and salt and pepper. Beat one of the eggs and stir into the mixture. Press into the mushrooms.

2 Preheat the oven to 200°C (400°F/Gas 6). Cut the pastry into quarters and cut a third off each. Roll out the thirds to rounds about 2cm (¾in) larger in diameter than the mushrooms. Line a baking sheet with baking parchment, lay the rounds on it, and place a stuffed mushroom in the centre of each. Beat the second egg and brush the edges with it.

3 Roll out the remaining pastry to rounds about 8cm (3in) larger than the mushrooms. Place the pastry over and press the edges to seal. Knock up and flute the edges with the back of a knife, then brush all over with beaten egg. Make a hole in the centre of each to allow steam to escape. Make leaves out of pastry trimmings, if liked, and arrange on top. Brush with the remaining egg. Bake in the oven for 40 minutes, or until puffy and golden and the mushrooms are cooked through.

4 Meanwhile, make the sauce. Heat the sunflower oil in a saucepan and add the chestnut mushrooms, finely chopped portobello mushroom stalks, and garlic. Cook, stirring, over a medium heat for about 3 minutes until tender and the liquid has evaporated.

5 Add the cider and boil for 2 minutes until reduced by half. Stir in the cream, thyme, and 6 tbsp water. Simmer for 3 minutes until reduced and thickened, stirring. Season with salt and pepper. Transfer the pies to plates, garnish with parsley, and serve with the sauce.

Leek, sage, walnut, and tomato tartlets

SERVES 4   PREPARATION **30 MINS, PLUS CHILLING**   TO COOK **15 MINS**

Serve these pretty tartlets with new potatoes and a crisp green salad. The crispy sage leaves add an extra dimension, but can be omitted if preferred.

INGREDIENTS

500g pack puff pastry,
  thawed if frozen
60g (2oz) butter
4 leeks, cut into thick slices
12 cherry tomatoes, halved
60g (2oz) walnut pieces,
  roughly chopped
1 tbsp chopped sage, plus
  a small handful of sage
  leaves, to garnish
salt and freshly ground
  black pepper
2 eggs, beaten
4 tbsp mayonnaise
sunflower oil, for frying

1 Cut the puff pastry into quarters and roll out to rectangles of about 15 × 18cm (6 × 7in). Place on 2 baking sheets lined with baking parchment. Score a line about 2cm (¾in) from each edge of the rectangles, taking care not to cut right through the pastry. This will form the rims of the tartlets. Chill for at least 30 minutes.

2 Meanwhile, make the filling. Melt the butter in a saucepan. Add the leeks and cook gently, stirring, for 2 minutes to soften slightly, but not brown. Reduce the heat, cover, and cook gently for 4 minutes until the leeks are soft, but still bright green and holding their shape. Tip into a bowl and set aside to cool, then add the tomatoes, walnuts, sage, and salt and pepper.

3 Preheat the oven to 200°C (400°F/Gas 6). Brush a little of the beaten egg around the rims of each tartlet. Beat the remainder with the mayonnaise and stir into the leek mixture. Spoon into the centres of the tartlets, leaving the rims free and making sure each tartlet gets a good mixture of leeks, walnuts, and tomatoes. Bake in the oven for about 20 minutes until the centres are set and the edges puffy and golden.

4 Meanwhile, heat about 1cm (½in) oil until hot, but not smoking. Put the sage leaves in a slotted spoon and lower into the hot oil. Cook for a few seconds, just until they stop sizzling and are bright green. Remove immediately and drain on kitchen paper. Scatter a few crispy leaves over each tartlet before serving.

Cheese and asparagus turnovers

MAKES 9 **PREPARATION 20 MINS** TO COOK **20–25 MINS**

These flaky, crumbly parcels are perfect for a light lunch or picnic on a sunny summer's day. Using ready-made pastry makes the preparation quick and easy.

INGREDIENTS

salt and freshly ground
  black pepper
100g (3½oz) asparagus spears,
  cut into 1cm (½in) strips
50g (1¾oz) mature Cheddar
  cheese, grated
3 tbsp snipped chives
500g ready-made puff pastry
plain flour, for dusting
1 egg, beaten, to glaze
sweet paprika, for dusting
salad leaves, to serve

1 Bring a small pan of salted water to the boil and blanch the asparagus spears for 2 minutes. Drain and refresh in cold water. Drain again and cool. Mix the asparagus with the cheese, chives, and plenty of pepper. Set aside.

2 Carefully roll out the pastry on a lightly floured surface to form a 30cm (12in) square, 5mm (¼in) in thickness. Trim the edges, then cut out 9 equal squares. Brush the edges of each square with water. Divide the asparagus filling between the squares, heaping it over one diagonal half of each. Fold the pastry over the filling and pinch the edges together to seal. Use a knife to flute and crimp the edges together.

3 Place the triangles well apart on a large, lightly greased baking sheet. Make a steam hole in the top of each, then glaze with beaten egg and dust with paprika. Bake for 20–25 minutes, or until golden and risen. Serve warm or cold with salad leaves.

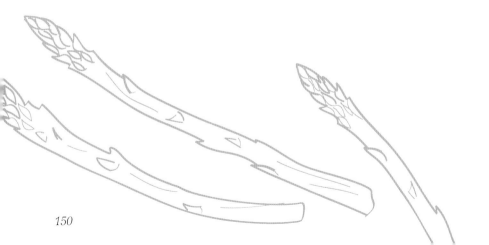

Spanakopita

SERVES 6   PREPARATION **20 MINS**   TO COOK **1 HR**

This is a **classic pie, filled with spinach, feta, and a hint of nutmeg**. Brushing the filo with butter between layers gives a really crisp, golden finish when baked.

1 Preheat the oven to 200°C (400°F/Gas 6). Heat the oil in a large frying pan, add the onion, and cook for 2–3 minutes. Season with salt and pepper. In a separate large pan, cook the spinach in 4 batches of 250g (9oz) each on a low heat for 4–5 minutes until it wilts. Remove and set aside.

2 In a bowl, stir together the feta, nutmeg, and dill, and season with more pepper. Add the eggs and combine. Squeeze any excess water from the spinach, then add this and the onion to the feta mixture and mix.

3 Brush a 1.4 litre (2½ pint) shallow rectangular dish with a little of the butter. Line with 1 sheet of filo and brush again. Lay the second sheet at right angles to the first and brush again with butter. Repeat with a third sheet at right angles again.

4 Fill the dish with the spinach mixture. Fold the edges of the filo over the top. Lay one of the remaining sheets of filo on top of the dish, folding the edges underneath so it fits the top of the dish. Brush with butter and lay another sheet on top folded the same way, then the final sheet. Brush the top with any remaining butter. Place the pie on a baking sheet.

5 Bake in the oven for about 20–25 minutes or until crisp and golden brown. Remove from the oven and leave to cool for 5–10 minutes before serving with a tomato salad.

INGREDIENTS

1 tbsp olive oil
½ onion, very finely chopped
salt and freshly ground
   black pepper
1kg (2¼lb) spinach
250g (9oz) feta cheese,
   crumbled
pinch of grated nutmeg
handful of dill, finely chopped
3 eggs
30g (1oz) butter, melted
6 sheets filo pastry
tomato salad, to serve

Four ways with
Peppers

Red pepper salad ▷

TAKES 35 mins **SERVES** 4

Heat 3 tbsp **olive oil** in a large frying pan. Add
6 **red peppers**, deseeded and cut into large strips,
and 2 finely chopped **garlic cloves**. Fry over a low
heat for 5 minutes, stirring, then add 250g (9oz)
ripe **tomatoes**, skinned, deseeded, and chopped.
Increase the heat, bring to simmering point, then
reduce to low, cover, and cook for 12–15 minutes.
Stir in 2 tbsp chopped **parsley**, season with **salt**
and freshly ground **black pepper**, and cook for
2 minutes. Transfer the peppers to a serving dish.
Add 1 tbsp **sherry vinegar** to the pan, increase
the heat, and simmer for 5–7 minutes. Pour the
sauce over the peppers and allow to cool.

◁ Pasta with roasted peppers

TAKES 35 mins **SERVES** 4

Roast and skin 6 **red peppers** (see p44) and
cut into strips. Melt a knob of **butter** with
3 tbsp **olive oil** in a frying pan and gently fry
2 chopped **garlic cloves** together with 1 **red
chilli** and 1 **green chilli**, deseeded and chopped,
for 2 minutes to soften, but not brown. Add a
generous pinch of **dried oregano** and 1 tbsp
thyme leaves. Cook 350g (12oz) **dried penne**
according to the packet instructions. Drain,
reserving a little of the cooking water. Return to
the pan, add the pepper mixture, and toss gently
with 25g (scant 1oz) grated **Pecorino cheese**.
Serve drizzled with **chilli oil**.

Peppers become sweeter as they ripen from green, through yellow and orange, to red. If you **buy them when glossy and firm**, they will store in the fridge for up to two weeks, but use them within 24 hours once cut.

Roasted mixed pepper bruschetta ▶

TAKES 1 hr   **SERVES** 4

Remove the seeds from 1 **red pepper** and 1 **yellow pepper**. Then slice the flesh into strips and add to a frying pan with a little **olive oil**. Season with **salt** and freshly ground **black pepper**. Cook until the peppers begin to soften. Increase the heat, add a drop of **balsamic vinegar**, and cook for a couple of minutes more. Toast 4 **ciabatta** slices. Peel and cut 1 **garlic clove** in half. Rub the cut side over each slice. Spoon the pepper mixture onto the bread slices and serve hot, garnished with a scattering of **basil** leaves.

◀ Red pepper and walnut dip

TAKES 50 mins   **SERVES** 8

Heat 90ml (3fl oz) **olive oil** in a heavy-based frying pan over a low heat. Add 1 sliced **onion**, then sweat gently for 5 minutes until soft and translucent. Tip in 4 **red peppers**, deseeded and sliced, and cook for about 30 minutes until soft, stirring regularly. Stir in 2 crushed **garlic cloves** and cook for a further 30 seconds, or until the garlic has turned white. Transfer the pepper mixture to a blender or food processor. Add 125g (4½oz) toasted and chopped **walnuts** and grated zest and juice of 1 **lemon**, then blend to a chunky purée. Serve with bread or crudités, such as carrot or cucumber batons, for dipping.

Mediterranean vegetable and feta filo pie

SERVES 4   **PREPARATION 35 MINS**   **TO COOK 25 MINS**

This pie is delicious hot or cold. Brush the layers of filo with olive oil instead of butter if preferred – although the butter gives a crisper finish to the dish.

INGREDIENTS

2 tbsp olive oil
1 red onion, chopped
1 garlic clove, crushed
1 red pepper, deseeded
   and cut into small chunks
1 green pepper, deseeded
   and cut into small chunks
1 aubergine, halved
   lengthways and sliced
1 large courgette, sliced
4 tomatoes, chopped
1 tsp dried oregano
small handful of pitted black
   olives, halved
salt and freshly ground
   black pepper
50g (1¾oz) butter, melted
6 sheets filo pastry
200g (7oz) feta cheese, diced
green salad, to serve

1 Heat the oil in a large saucepan. Add the onion and garlic along with the vegetables and fry, stirring, for about 3 minutes until slightly softened. Cover, reduce the heat, and cook gently for 20 minutes, stirring occasionally.

2 Stir in the oregano, olives, and a little salt and pepper (the cheese and olives will be salty when added). Set aside to cool.

3 Preheat the oven to 200°C (400°F/Gas 6). Brush a 1.4 litre (2½ pint) shallow rectangular dish with a little of the butter. Line with a sheet of filo and brush again. Lay a second sheet at right angles to the first and brush again with butter. Repeat with a third sheet at right angles again.

4 Fill the dish with the vegetable mixture and scatter the cheese over, pressing it into the surface. Fold the edges of the filo over the top. Lay one of the remaining sheets of filo on top of the dish, folding the edges underneath so it fits the top of the dish. Brush with butter and lay another sheet on top folded the same way, then the final sheet. Brush the top with any remaining butter. Place the pie on a baking sheet.

5 Bake in the oven for about 20–25 minutes, or until crisp and golden brown. Remove from the oven and leave to cool for 5–10 minutes before serving with a green salad.

Tarts, pies, and parcels
Vegetable samosas

SERVES 4   PREPARATION **45 MINS, PLUS RESTING AND COOLING**   TO COOK **35–40 MINS**

Serve these Indian pastries hot or cold. In India they would be fried in ghee, a clarified butter that can be heated to a high temperature, but oil works equally well.

INGREDIENTS

350g (12oz) plain flour, plus extra for dusting

salt and freshly ground black pepper

9 tbsp sunflower oil or ghee, plus extra for frying

450g (1lb) potatoes, scrubbed

225g (8oz) cauliflower, chopped into small pieces

175g (6oz) peas, thawed if frozen

2 shallots, sliced

2 tbsp curry paste

2 tbsp chopped coriander

1 tbsp lemon juice

1 To make the pastry, sift the flour into a bowl with ½ tsp salt. Stir in 6 tbsp oil or ghee and gradually add 120ml (4fl oz) warm water, mixing to make a dough. Knead the dough on a floured surface until smooth. Wrap in cling film and leave to rest for at least 30 minutes.

2 To make the filling, cook the potatoes in a saucepan of boiling water until tender. Drain and cool, then peel and chop into small pieces. Blanch the cauliflower florets in a pan of boiling water for 2–3 minutes, or until just tender, then drain. If using fresh peas, blanch them with the cauliflower.

3 Heat the remaining oil in a large frying pan and fry the shallots for 3–4 minutes, stirring frequently, until soft. Add the potatoes, cauliflower, peas, curry paste, coriander, and lemon juice, and cook over a low heat for 2–3 minutes, stirring occasionally. Set aside to cool.

4 Divide the dough into 8 equal pieces. Roll them out so each forms an 18cm (7in) round. Cut each round in half and shape into a cone, dampening the edges to seal. Spoon a little of the filling into each cone, dampen the top edge of the dough, and press down over the filling to enclose it. Repeat with the rest of the dough and filling.

5 Heat oil for deep-frying to 180°C (350°F), or until a cube of day-old bread browns in 30 seconds. Fry the samosas in batches for 3–4 minutes, or until golden brown on both sides. Drain on kitchen paper and serve hot or cold.

Sweetcorn and pepper empanadas

MAKES 24   **PREPARATION 45 MINS, PLUS CHILLING**   TO COOK **40–50 MINS**

These Spanish pastries make versatile snacks. For a main meal, make fewer, larger pies, using a tea plate as a guide to cut out the dough. The baking time is the same.

1 To make the pastry, sift the flour into a large mixing bowl with ½ tsp salt. Add the butter and rub in with your fingertips until it resembles fine breadcrumbs. Add the beaten eggs with 4–6 tbsp water and combine to form a dough. Cover with cling film and chill for 30 minutes.

2 Heat the oil in a frying pan, add the onion, and fry for 3 minutes until softened. Add the green pepper and fry for a further 3 minutes, stirring frequently. Add the tomatoes, tomato purée, and paprika. Season with salt and pepper, partially cover and simmer, stirring occasionally, for 5 minutes until pulpy. Stir in the chopped egg and parsley.

3 Preheat the oven to 190°C (375°F/Gas 5). Roll out the pastry to a thickness of 3mm (⅛in). Cut out 24 rounds with a 9cm (3½ in) round pastry cutter. Put a heaped tsp of the mixture on each, then brush the edges with water, fold over, and pinch together.

4 Place the empanadas on an oiled baking tray and brush with some beaten egg. Bake for 25–30 minutes, or until golden brown, and serve warm.

INGREDIENTS

450g (1lb) plain flour, plus extra for dusting
salt and freshly ground black pepper
85g (3oz) butter, diced
2 eggs, beaten, plus extra to glaze
1 tbsp olive oil
1 onion, finely chopped
1 green pepper, deseeded and finely chopped
2 tomatoes, chopped
2 tsp tomato purée
1 tsp sweet paprika
2 hard-boiled eggs, chopped
2 tbsp finely chopped parsley

Grills and bakes

Grilled marinated halloumi on seeded vegetable ribbons

SERVES 4   PREPARATION **20 MINS, PLUS MARINATING**   TO COOK **6 MINS**

Salty halloumi, fragrant with herbs and garlic, marries beautifully with sweet-tasting vegetables here. Take care not to overcook the veg – it should retain some bite.

INGREDIENTS

1 lime
8 tbsp olive oil
1 tsp crushed dried chillies
1 tsp dried oregano
½ tsp dried mint
1 garlic clove, crushed
salt and freshly ground
   black pepper
250g (9oz) block halloumi
   cheese, cut into 8 slices
Mediterranean flatbreads
   (khobez), and a dish each
   of olives and pickled
   chillies, to serve

For the vegetable ribbons

2 thin parsnips, peeled
   but left whole
2 large carrots, peeled
   but left whole
2 courgettes, trimmed
   but left whole
1 tbsp sesame oil
2 tbsp black onion seeds
2 tbsp sesame seeds

1 Put 8 wooden skewers in cold water to soak. Finely grate the zest of the lime into a shallow dish. Squeeze the juice into a separate dish. Whisk 6 tbsp olive oil into the zest with half the lime juice, chillies, herbs, garlic, and plenty of pepper. Add the cheese slices, turn to coat completely, and leave to marinate for several hours or overnight, turning once or twice.

2 Pare the vegetables with a potato peeler, holding them firmly at each side and turning at intervals to shave them all around. There will be a central piece you cannot pare, which can be set aside to use for soup.

3 Heat the remaining olive oil in a large frying pan or wok. Add all the vegetables and stir-fry for 2 minutes until beginning to soften. Cover and cook for a further 2 minutes until tender, but still with a little crunch. Add the sesame oil, remaining lime juice, onion seeds, and sesame seeds, and toss well. Season lightly with salt and pepper. Remove from the heat.

4 Preheat an oiled, flat griddle pan or grill rack. Remove the cheese from the marinade and thread a piece on each of the soaked wooden skewers. Griddle for 1 minute on each side, pressing down with a fish slice, until charred brown in places. Place on a plate and drizzle the remaining marinade over.

5 Toss the ribbons over a high heat once more to heat through. Serve the vegetable ribbons with the cheese sticks, Mediterranean flatbreads, olives, and pickled chillies.

Grilled stuffed romano peppers with chilli and cheese

SERVES 4   PREPARATION **15 MINS**   TO COOK **20 MINS**

When available, baby romano peppers stuffed like this make a great starter (use eight and halve the filling). The large peppers are enough for a light main meal.

INGREDIENTS

4 large romano peppers
250g (9oz) medium-fat
   soft cheese
175g (6oz) mature Cheddar
   cheese, grated
60g (2oz) fresh breadcrumbs
1–2 green chillies,
   finely chopped
2 tbsp chopped parsley, plus
   extra to garnish
2 tbsp chopped coriander
salt and freshly ground
   black pepper
olive oil
crusty bread and mixed
   salad, to serve

1 Preheat the grill. Cut the stalk ends off the peppers and discard. Split them down one side and carefully remove any remaining seeds and pith, taking care not to break the peppers.

2 Mix the cheeses with the breadcrumbs, chillies, herbs, and salt and pepper to taste. Divide the cheese mixture among the peppers, spreading it evenly inside them.

3 Place the peppers on oiled foil in the grill pan. Brush with oil. Grill for 8–10 minutes on each side until the cheese is melting and bubbling and the peppers are soft, but not blackened.

4 Carefully transfer to plates (including any lovely gooey bits that have oozed out). Drizzle with a little more oil and sprinkle with a little parsley to garnish. Serve immediately with plenty of crusty bread and a mixed salad.

Grilled avocado with semi-dried tomato dressing

SERVES 4   PREPARATION **10 MINS**   TO COOK **8 MINS**

Cooked avocados are delicious, as long as they are ripe – under-ripe ones will taste bitter. Ricotta cheese can be substituted for cottage cheese in this recipe.

1 Halve the avocados and remove the stones. Brush the cut surfaces and the skin with olive oil.

2 For the dressing, whisk the olive oil with 2 tbsp tomato oil, white balsamic condiment, garlic, and some salt and pepper, then stir in the semi-dried tomatoes and basil. Set aside.

3 Preheat a griddle pan. Mix the cheese with the olives and set aside. Place the avocados cut-side down on the griddle and cook for 3 minutes until striped brown, pressing down gently with a fish slice for even cooking of the cut side. Turn the avocados over and cook for a further 2–3 minutes until hot through. It does not matter if the skins burn a little, but take care not to overcook the avocados as they will become unpleasantly mushy.

4 Place the avocado halves on serving plates and spoon the cool cheese into the centres. Spoon the dressing over and serve with walnut or multigrain bread and a watercress and orange salad.

INGREDIENTS

4 large or 8 small
   ripe avocados
2 tbsp olive oil, plus
   extra for brushing
6 semi-dried tomatoes in oil,
   drained and chopped,
   oil reserved
1 tbsp white
   balsamic condiment
1 small garlic clove, crushed
salt and freshly ground
   black pepper
2 tbsp chopped basil
250g (9oz) plain cottage
   cheese, or flavoured
   with chives
2 tbsp black olives, chopped
walnut or multigrain bread,
   and watercress and orange
   salad, to serve

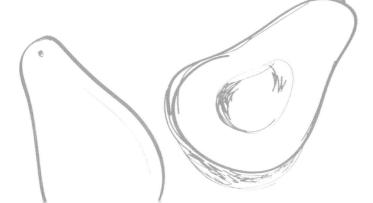

Mixed vegetable cottage pie with swede crust

SERVES 4   PREPARATION **30 MINS**   TO COOK **40 MINS**

This rich, intensely flavoured variation on a family favourite will please even the most dedicated meat-eater. Parsnips may be substituted for the swede in the topping.

INGREDIENTS

1 tbsp sunflower oil
1 onion, finely chopped
115g (4oz) white
   mushrooms, sliced
2 carrots, grated
2 turnips, grated
60g (2oz) shelled fresh
   or thawed frozen peas
2 × 400g cans borlotti beans,
   rinsed and drained
450ml (15fl oz) vegetable stock
1 tbsp soy sauce
1 tbsp mushroom ketchup
   or Worcestershire sauce
1 tsp dried mixed herbs
salt and freshly ground
   black pepper
4 tbsp plain flour
1 small swede, cut into
   small chunks
450g (1lb) potatoes, peeled
   and cut into small chunks
knob of butter
4 tbsp milk
grated nutmeg
60g (2oz) strong Cheddar
   cheese, grated
shredded greens, to serve

1 Heat the oil in a large saucepan. Add the onion and fry, stirring, for 3 minutes until lightly golden. Add the mushrooms, carrots, turnips, peas, and borlotti beans. Stir in the stock, soy sauce, mushroom ketchup, herbs, and salt and pepper to taste. Bring to the boil, reduce the heat, cover, and simmer gently for 10 minutes until the vegetables are tender. Blend the flour with 4 tbsp water. Stir into the pan and cook, stirring, for 2 minutes to thicken.

2 While the other vegetables are simmering, cook the swede and potato in salted boiling water for 15 minutes or until tender. Drain and return to the pan over a low heat to dry out slightly. Mash with the butter, milk, a generous grating of nutmeg, and a generous grinding of pepper. Beat well with a wooden spoon until smooth.

3 Preheat the oven to 190°C (375°F/Gas 5). Spoon the mixture into a 1.7 litre (3 pint) ovenproof dish or 4 individual dishes. Top with the swede mash and fluff up with a fork. Sprinkle the cheese over and bake in the oven for about 40 minutes until golden. Serve hot with some shredded greens.

Watercress and beetroot roulade with smooth cheese sauce

SERVES 4   PREPARATION **30 MINS**   TO COOK **18 MINS**

This light and luscious roulade is also **delicious served cold with dill-flavoured mayonnaise**. For an alternative filling, the chunky tomato sauce on p133 is ideal.

INGREDIENTS

1 bunch watercress,
  finely chopped
2 tbsp chopped parsley
2 tbsp grated Parmesan
  cheese, plus extra
  for dusting
4 eggs, separated

For the cheese sauce

2 tbsp plain flour
300ml (10fl oz) milk
15g (½oz) butter
½ tsp English mustard
60g (2oz) Cheddar
  cheese, grated
salt and freshly ground
  black pepper

For the filling

100g (3½oz) crème fraîche
1 spring onion, finely chopped
2 cooked beetroot (approx.
  125g/4½oz), finely chopped
1 tbsp chopped dill, plus
  extra to garnish (optional)
squeeze of lemon juice
grated nutmeg

1 First, make the sauce. Put the flour in a small saucepan. Whisk in the milk, then add the butter. Bring to the boil and cook for 2 minutes, whisking constantly, until thickened. Stir in the mustard and Cheddar cheese until melted and add salt and pepper to taste. Cover with a circle of damp greaseproof or baking parchment to prevent a skin forming and keep warm.

2 To make the filling, mix the ingredients together in a small saucepan with a generous grating of nutmeg and a little salt and pepper. Heat through, stirring gently. Keep warm.

3 Preheat the oven to 200°C (400°F/Gas 6). Grease an 18 × 28cm (7 × 11in) Swiss roll tin and line with baking parchment.

4 Put the watercress in a bowl, then add the parsley and Parmesan. Beat in the egg yolks and some salt and pepper. Whisk the egg whites until stiff and fold into the watercress mix with a metal spoon. Transfer to the prepared tin and smooth the surface. Bake in the oven for about 8 minutes until risen and just firm to the touch.

5 Place a clean sheet of baking parchment on a clean tea towel on the work surface. Dust the parchment with a little grated Parmesan. Turn out the roulade onto the prepared paper, then loosen the cooking paper and remove gently.

6 Quickly spread the roulade with the beetroot filling, leaving a small border all around. Roll up, using the parchment to help. Transfer to a serving plate and garnish with some chopped dill, if using. Cut in slices and serve with the cheese sauce.

Four ways with
Aubergines

Aubergine and goat's cheese crostini ▶

TAKES 30 mins **SERVES** 4

Preheat the oven to 180°C (350°F/Gas 4). Brush 12 slices of **French bread** on both sides with **olive oil**. Toast for 10 minutes. Halve 1 **garlic clove** and rub the cut side over each slice. Slice 1 **aubergine** into 5mm (¼in) thick rounds, brush each side with oil, and griddle both sides until cooked. Quarter the aubergine slices and place in a bowl. Add 1 tbsp olive oil, 2 tbsp chopped **mint**, and 1 tbsp **balsamic vinegar**. Toss and season with **salt** and freshly ground **black pepper**. Spread the crostini with 60g (2oz) **soft goat's cheese**, top with aubergine, and serve.

◀ Steamed aubergine salad

TAKES 35 mins **SERVES** 6

Cut 2 medium peeled **aubergines** into 2cm (¾in) cubes and steam, covered, for 10 minutes. When cool, squeeze gently to extract as much water as possible. In a bowl, combine 60g (2oz) crumbled **soft goat's cheese**, 2 ripe **tomatoes**, deseeded and diced, 1 small finely diced **red onion**, a handful of finely chopped **flat-leaf parsley**, 60g (2oz) lightly toasted and roughly chopped **walnuts**, and 1 tbsp lightly toasted **sesame seeds**. For the dressing, whisk together 1 crushed **garlic clove**, 4 tbsp **walnut oil**, and the juice of 1 **lemon**. Drizzle over the salad, season with **salt** and freshly ground **black pepper**, and toss to mix.

The aubergines most commonly available are the deep purple variety – but you may also find **the prettily mottled Rosa Bianca**, the round Prosperosa, which is ideal for stuffing, or **crispy-textured East Asian varieties**.

Tomato and aubergine confit ▶

TAKES 15 mins, plus standing **SERVES** 6

Heat 2 tbsp **olive oil** and 5 tbsp **sunflower oil** in a large frying pan over a medium-high heat until the oil begins to smoke. Add 300g (10oz) **aubergines**, cut into 7.5cm (3in) batons, and fry, stirring often, for 3 minutes, or until golden brown. Drain. Add 4 tbsp **garlic-infused oil** to the pan, then add 125g (4½oz) **cherry tomatoes**, halved. Cook for 2 minutes, or until softened. Place the batons in a bowl. Add 10 torn **basil leaves** and the tomatoes and mix gently. Cover and leave to infuse for up to 1 hour in a warm place. Season with **salt** and freshly ground **black pepper**. Serve warm.

◀ Grilled aubergines with pomegranate vinaigrette

TAKES 20 mins **SERVES** 6

To make the vinaigrette, whisk together 6 tbsp **olive oil**, 3 tbsp **pomegranate syrup**, and 3 tbsp chopped **coriander**, and season with **salt** and freshly ground **black pepper**. Set aside. Preheat a griddle pan over a high heat. Cut 3 large **aubergines** into 1cm (½in) thick slices. Brush both sides of the aubergine slices with olive oil, season, then griddle both sides until tender. Layer the aubergines and 2 very finely sliced **shallots** in a serving dish and pour over the vinaigrette. Scatter with **pomegranate seeds** and serve.

Lentil, mushroom, and egg loaf with celeriac remoulade

SERVES 8   **PREPARATION 30 MINS**   **TO COOK 1 HR**

This loaf is **best made the day before eating** so that it has time to cool properly and firm up. Serve with baby plum tomatoes and jacket potatoes.

INGREDIENTS

4 savoy cabbage leaves
2 tbsp olive oil, plus extra
   for greasing
knob of butter
2 shallots, finely chopped
115g (4oz) crimini
   mushrooms, sliced
2 × 410g cans green lentils,
   rinsed and drained
115g (4oz) fresh breadcrumbs
2 tbsp chopped thyme
2 tbsp chopped parsley
1 tbsp mushroom ketchup
   or Worcestershire sauce
1 tsp ground coriander
salt and freshly ground
   black pepper
1 egg, beaten
3 hard-boiled eggs, shelled

For the remoulade
4 tbsp mayonnaise
4 tbsp crème fraîche
2 tsp grated horseradish or
   hot horseradish relish
2 tsp white balsamic condiment
1 small celeriac

1 Cut the thick central stalks out of 4 large outer leaves from the cabbage. Blanch the leaves in boiling water for 2 minutes, then drain, rinse with cold water, and drain again. Dry on kitchen paper. Oil a 900g (2lb) loaf tin. Line with overlapping cabbage leaves, outer sides against the tin and stalk ends upwards, allowing enough to hang over the top edge all around to form a wrap for the loaf.

2 Heat the oil and butter in a large pan. Add the shallots and fry, stirring, for 2 minutes. Add the mushrooms and fry for 2 minutes, stirring. Remove from the heat. Add the lentils, breadcrumbs, herbs, ketchup, coriander, and salt and pepper. Mix with the beaten egg.

3 Preheat the oven to 190°C (375°F/Gas 5). Spoon half the lentil mixture into the tin and press down. Lay the boiled eggs down the centre, end-to-end, and press gently into the mixture. Top with the remaining mixture, pressing gently. Fold the overhanging leaves over.

4 Cover the tin with oiled foil, twisting it under the rim to secure. Bake in the oven for 1 hour until just firm. Remove from the oven and leave to cool, then weigh down with cans of food and chill to firm.

5 An hour before serving, make the remoulade. Blend the mayonnaise, crème fraîche, horseradish, and balsamic condiment in a bowl. Peel the celeriac, slice thinly, and cut into thin matchsticks, or shred in a food processor. Place immediately in the dressing and toss well. Season with salt and pepper. Cover the bowl with cling film and chill.

6 Turn the loaf out onto a serving dish. Serve sliced with the remoulade. Any leftovers are delicious with pickles and crusty bread for another meal.

Courgette and carrot pavé

SERVES 4   **PREPARATION** **15 MINS**   TO COOK **40 MINS**

This baked slab, or pavé, of lightly spiced vegetables is delicious hot or cold. It can also be served in little squares as bite-sized snacks or canapés.

1 Preheat the oven to 190°C (375°F/Gas 5). Mix all the ingredients except the sesame seeds in a bowl until thoroughly blended.

2 Transfer to an oiled 18 × 28cm (7 × 11in) shallow baking tin. Sprinkle liberally with the sesame seeds. Bake in the oven for 40 minutes until golden and firm to the touch.

3 Cool for 5 minutes, then cut into quarters. Place each pavé on a serving plate. Garnish with sprigs of parsley and drizzle the plates with a splash of sesame oil. Serve with new potatoes and a mixed salad.

INGREDIENTS

1 large onion, finely chopped
2 large courgettes, grated
2 large carrots, grated
115g (4oz) Cheddar
   cheese, grated
115g (4oz) plain flour
1 tsp ground cumin
1 tsp dried mixed herbs
1 tsp crushed dried chillies
salt and freshly ground
   black pepper
6 tbsp sunflower oil
5 eggs, beaten
2 tbsp sesame oil, plus
   extra for drizzling
3–4 tbsp sesame seeds
a few sprigs of parsley,
   to garnish
new potatoes and mixed
   salad, to serve

Potato and mixed nut moussaka

SERVES 4–6   **PREPARATION 45 MINS**   TO COOK **45 MINS**

A simple, rustic dish, this is delicious served with a Greek-style salad, topped with cubes of feta cheese, and drizzled with olive oil and red wine vinegar.

INGREDIENTS

675g (1½lb) potatoes,
  scrubbed and cut
  into 5mm (¼in) slices
2 tbsp olive oil, plus extra
  for greasing
1 large onion, chopped
2 garlic cloves, crushed
2 courgettes, sliced
1 green pepper, deseeded
  and chopped
400g can chopped tomatoes
400g can cannellini beans,
  rinsed and drained
115g (4oz) chopped
  mixed nuts
2 tbsp tomato purée
2 tsp dried oregano
1 tsp ground cinnamon
3 tbsp sliced black olives
salt and freshly ground
  black pepper
400g (14oz) crème fraîche
2 eggs
50g (1¾oz) Parmesan
  cheese, grated

1 Cook the potatoes in boiling water for about 5 minutes, or until tender, but still holding their shape. Drain, rinse with cold water, and drain again.

2 Heat the oil in a large saucepan and add the onion, garlic, courgettes, and green pepper. Fry, stirring, for 5 minutes, turning the vegetables over as they soften slightly. Add the tomatoes, beans, nuts, tomato purée, 1 tsp oregano, cinnamon, olives, and plenty of pepper. Bring to the boil, reduce the heat, and simmer for about 15 minutes until the vegetables are tender and the sauce is thick, stirring occasionally.

3 Preheat the oven to 180°C (350°F/Gas 4). Put half the vegetable mixture into a lightly oiled 2-litre (3½-pint) rectangular ovenproof dish and spread it out. Top with a layer of half the potatoes. Repeat the layers with the remaining vegetable mixture and potatoes.

4 Beat the crème fraîche with the eggs, remaining oregano, Parmesan, and some salt and pepper. Spread over the top of the potatoes. Bake in the oven for about 45 minutes until the top is golden and set. Leave to cool for a while to intensify the flavours, and serve warm.

Carrot, onion, and Stilton hot dogs

MAKES 12   PREPARATION **20 MINS, PLUS CHILLING**   TO COOK **5 MINS**

These hot dogs can be made in advance and kept in the fridge for several days before cooking. They are **equally good with Cheddar cheese instead of Stilton**.

INGREDIENTS

knob of butter
1 onion, finely chopped
4 carrots, grated
350g (12oz) rolled oats
100g (3½oz) plain flour,
   plus extra for dusting
175g (6oz) crumbled
   Stilton cheese (or similar
   crumbly blue cheese)
2 tbsp tomato purée
1 tbsp soy sauce
2 tbsp mushroom ketchup
   or Worcestershire sauce
1 tsp dried mixed herbs
2 tbsp chopped parsley
2 large eggs, beaten
salt and freshly ground
   black pepper
sunflower oil, for frying
hot dog rolls, American
   mild mustard, and
   a salad, to serve

For the garnish
knob of butter
4 large onions, halved
   and thinly sliced
4 ripe tomatoes, deseeded
   and chopped

1 Heat the butter in a saucepan. Add the onion and carrots and fry gently for 2 minutes, stirring. Remove from the heat and transfer to a food processor. Add the remaining ingredients and plenty of salt and pepper, then blend well. Chill the mixture for about 30 minutes, if necessary, to firm before shaping.

2 With floured hands, shape the mixture into 12 long sausages (like slightly fat hot dogs). Chill for at least 30 minutes to firm.

3 Meanwhile, make the garnish. Melt the butter in the same saucepan, add the onions, and fry, stirring, for 2 minutes. Reduce the heat, cover, and cook gently for 10 minutes until soft and lightly golden, stirring occasionally. Stir in the tomatoes and cook for 1 minute. Season to taste.

4 Grill the sausages, brushed with a little oil, or shallow-fry in a little hot oil for about 5 minutes, turning occasionally, until golden brown all over.

5 Place the sausages in the split rolls and add the onion and tomato garnish and a squeeze of American mustard. Serve with a salad on the side.

Pestos, pickles, salsas, and dips

Roasted red pepper, almond, and chilli pesto

MAKES 1 SMALL JAR (approx. 175g/6oz)   **PREPARATION** **10 MINS**

As well as stirring it through pasta, **try spreading this zingy pesto on bruschetta** and topping it with tomatoes and basil. It also works well on pizza bases.

INGREDIENTS

1 red pepper, roasted
  (see p44), deseeded
  and roughly chopped
4 semi-dried tomatoes
  in oil, drained
1–2 fat red chillies, deseeded
  and roughly chopped
2 garlic cloves, lightly crushed
30g (1oz) ground almonds
30g (1oz) grated
  Parmesan cheese
2 tbsp tomato oil from the jar
salt and freshly ground
  black pepper
4 tbsp extra virgin olive oil

1 Place the red pepper in a food processor with the semi-dried tomatoes, chillies, garlic, almonds, cheese, tomato oil, and a generous sprinkling of salt and pepper. Run the machine until well blended, stopping and scraping down the sides as necessary. With the machine running, trickle in 2 tbsp olive oil until you have a glistening paste.

2 Alternatively, put the red pepper, tomatoes, chillies, and garlic in a mortar and pound with a pestle. Gradually add the almonds and salt and pepper. Work in a little of the cheese, then add a little each of the tomato oil and olive oil. Continue until the cheese, tomato oil, and 2 tbsp olive oil are used up and you have a glistening paste.

3 Spoon into a clean, sterilized jar, top with the remaining olive oil to prevent air getting in, screw the lid on, and store in the refrigerator. Use within 2 weeks.

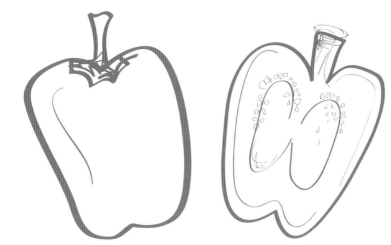

Indian-spiced vegetable chutney

MAKES 3 JARS (approx. 350g/12oz each)   PREPARATION **30 MINS**   TO COOK **2 HR 15 MINS**

A selection of vegetables simmered in Indian spices and vinegar give this colourful chutney its flavour. Add 1–2 finely chopped green chillies for heat.

INGREDIENTS

900g (2lb) butternut squash, seeds removed, peeled, and cut into bite-sized chunks

2 onions, finely chopped

225g (8oz) cooking apples, peeled, cored, and chopped

3 courgettes, halved lengthways and chopped

50g (1¾oz) ready-to-eat stoned dates, chopped

450ml (15fl oz) cider vinegar

2 tbsp medium or hot curry powder

1 tsp ground cumin

2.5cm (1in) piece fresh root ginger, grated or finely chopped

450g (1lb) granulated or light soft brown sugar

1 Put the squash, onions, cooking apples, courgettes, and dates in a preserving pan or a large, heavy-based, stainless-steel saucepan. Pour in the vinegar, add the spices and ginger, and mix well.

2 Bring the mixture to the boil, then reduce the heat and simmer for 40–45 minutes, or until the vegetables are soft, stirring occasionally.

3 Add the sugar, stir until it is dissolved, then continue to cook on a gentle simmer for 1–1½ hours, or until the chutney is thick and the liquid has been absorbed. Stir continuously near the end of the cooking time so that the chutney doesn't catch on the base of the pan.

4 Ladle into warmed sterilized jars with non-metallic vinegar-proof lids, making sure there are no air gaps. Cover each pot with a waxed paper disc, seal, and label.

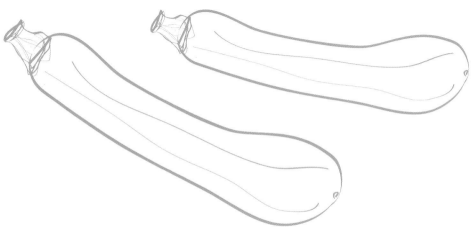

Pestos, pickles, salsas, and dips

Corn relish

MAKES 2 LARGE JARS (approx. 500g/1lb 2oz each)   PREPARATION **25 MINS**   TO COOK **20 MINS**

Made from diced fruit or vegetables, relish is part-pickle, part-chutney, but cooked for a shorter time than the latter. **It packs a tangy punch of flavour.**

1 Strip the kernels from the cobs using a sharp knife (see p39). Blanch them in a saucepan of boiling water for 2 minutes, then drain well.

2 Put the sweetcorn and the other ingredients in a saucepan, bring to the boil, and stir. Simmer gently, stirring, for 15–20 minutes.

3 Check the seasoning, then spoon into warmed sterilized jars. The relish should be a spoonable consistency and wetter than a chutney.

4 Seal with non-metallic or vinegar-proof lids, leave to cool, and label. Store in a cool, dark place. Once opened, store the jars in the fridge.

INGREDIENTS

4 sweetcorn cobs
2 peppers, green or red, deseeded and diced
2 celery sticks, finely sliced
1 red chilli, deseeded and sliced
1 onion, peeled and sliced
450ml (15fl oz) white wine vinegar
225g (8oz) caster sugar
2 tsp sea salt
2 tsp mustard powder
½ tsp ground turmeric

Onions

Onion confit ▶

TAKES 50 mins **MAKES** 750g (1lb 10oz)

Melt 30g (1oz) **butter** in a heavy-based saucepan.
Peel and finely slice 900g (2lb) **onions** and add
to the melted butter. Stir and cook for about
5 minutes, or until soft and translucent. Now
add 100g (3½ oz) **demerara sugar**, 3 tbsp
sherry vinegar, 1½ tbsp **crème de cassis**
(optional), and 2 tsp **salt**. Stir the ingredients
well and simmer, uncovered, for 30–40 minutes,
stirring occasionally so that the confit does not
stick to the pan or burn. To serve, try the confit
spread on bruschetta with grilled **goat's cheese**,
or in wraps with grated **Cheddar cheese**
and some salad.

◀ Onion bhajis

TAKES 30 mins **SERVES** 4

Mix together 225g (8oz) chopped **onions**,
115g (4oz) **besan** (gram flour), 2 tsp **cumin seeds**,
½ tsp **turmeric**, 1 tsp ground **coriander**, and
1 **green** or **red chilli**, deseeded and very finely
chopped. Add about 8 tbsp cold water to bind
the mixture to a thick batter. Heat **sunflower oil**
in a deep-fat fryer to 190°C (375°F). When hot,
place spoonfuls of the mixture, roughly the size
of golf balls, into the oil. Fry, turning occasionally,
until golden all over. Remove the bhajis using a
slotted spoon and drain. Return them to the pan
and quickly fry a second time until crisp and
golden brown all over. Drain and serve hot.

Most main-course dishes include onions, but **here they are the star ingredient**. Choose spring onions for salads and stir-fries, brown or white onions for general use, red ones for a sweeter flavour, and **shallots for a milder taste**.

Onion and almond soup ▶

TAKES 1 hr 10 mins **SERVES** 4

Add 100g (3½oz) **almonds** to boiling water, cover, and soak for 15 minutes. Slip off the skins. Whizz in a blender with 100ml (3½oz) hot **vegetable stock**. Fry ¼ tsp **nigella seeds** in 60g (2oz) **butter** for 1 minute. Add 4 diced **onions** and 1 chopped **red chilli**, cover, and cook for 25 minutes. Uncover and when the onions are golden, add 1 tsp **muscovado sugar**. Cook until it catches on the bottom. Add 2 tbsp **balsamic vinegar** and cook until sticky. Add 600ml (1 pint) stock and the almond paste; simmer for 20 minutes. Whizz in a blender. Return to the pan, add 120ml (4fl oz) **single cream**, and season. Reheat, garnish with fried sliced onion, and serve.

◀ Onion tart

TAKES 1 hr 10 mins **SERVES** 6

Preheat the oven to 200°C (400°F/Gas 6). Heat 1 tbsp **olive oil** in a non-stick frying pan, add 4 sliced **onions**, sweat gently for 15 minutes, remove from the heat, and stir in 1 tbsp **plain flour**. Add a little of 300ml (10fl oz) **milk** and stir. Return the pan to the heat and slowly stir in the milk. Add 1 tsp mild **paprika** and season with **salt** and freshly ground **black pepper**. Remove from the heat. Roll out 300g (10oz) **shortcrust pastry** and use to line a tart tin. Trim excess pastry and bake blind. Reduce the oven to 180°C (350°F/Gas 4). Spoon the onion mixture into the shell and top with 1 tsp **paprika**. Bake for 15–20 minutes. Serve.

Mexican tomato, onion, and coriander salsa

SERVES 4   PREPARATION **10 MINS, PLUS CHILLING**

This simple salsa is delicious with fajitas, tacos, and plain quesadillas, or just with corn tortilla chips as a nibble before a meal.

INGREDIENTS

1 large red onion,
  finely chopped
2–3 large tomatoes,
  finely chopped
1 large green chilli, such as
  jalapeño, deseeded and
  finely chopped
large handful of
  coriander, chopped
juice of 1 lime
salt and freshly ground
  black pepper

1 Mix all the vegetables with the coriander in a bowl. Add the lime juice and season with salt and pepper.

2 Cover with cling film and chill for at least 30 minutes to allow the flavours to develop before serving.

Yogurt, aubergine, and pine nut dip

SERVES 8–10   **PREPARATION** **15 MINS**   TO COOK **40 MINS**

This dip is also delicious with a pinch of cinnamon added as well as (or instead of) the cumin. It is great served with olives, and pickled chillies too.

INGREDIENTS

1 large aubergine
1 tbsp olive oil
2–3 tbsp tahini
2 garlic cloves, finely chopped
   or crushed
juice of 1 lemon, plus extra
   if needed
pinch of ground cumin
salt and freshly ground
   black pepper
pitta bread, to serve

1 Preheat the oven to 200°C (400°F/Gas 6). Pierce the aubergine a few times all over with a knife. Next, using your hands, rub the aubergine with oil. Roast in the oven for 30–40 minutes until it begins to char and the flesh is tender.

2 When the aubergine is cool enough to handle, peel off the skin and put the roasted flesh in a blender or food processor. Add the tahini, garlic, lemon juice, and cumin and blend to a purée.

3 Taste and season with salt and pepper, adding more lemon juice if needed. Blend again briefly. Spoon into a bowl or serving dish and serve with pitta bread.

Hummus

SERVES 8–10   **PREPARATION** **10 MINS**

Try this nutritious dip spread on spears of chicory, celery sticks, hollowed-out chunks of cucumber or, for a colourful effect, wedges of red pepper.

1 Put all the ingredients except the oil in a blender or food processor. Blend to a smooth purée.

2 With the motor running, gradually add the oil, a little at a time, until the hummus reaches the preferred consistency. Taste and season with salt, adding some more lemon juice if you like. Blend again. Serve as a dip with some warmed pitta bread.

INGREDIENTS

400g can chickpeas, drained and rinsed
2 garlic cloves, crushed
juice of 1 lemon, plus extra if needed
2–3 tbsp tahini
pinch of sweet paprika
salt
2–3 tbsp olive oil
pitta bread, to serve

Index

Page numbers in *italics* indicate descriptions of ingredients. Page numbers in **bold** indicate illustrated preparation techniques.

About the author

Carolyn Humphries has been a food writer and editor for more than 30 years. She started her career as a chef, but soon realised she preferred to create food for people to cook at home. After training as a journalist, she became a food writer for *Woman* magazine in the mid 1970s. She has since written for numerous magazines, and is the author of more than 60 books. With a passion for good food, she cares deeply about what we eat and where it comes from. She is dedicated to promoting healthy eating, encouraging everyone to buy local produce where possible, and to creating sumptuous recipes celebrating the best ingredients.

Acknowledgments

The author would like to thank: Dorling Kindersley for giving me the opportunity to write this book. As the years have gone by I have become more and more vegetarian orientated and this book has been the perfect opportunity to encourage more people to eat more veg and to celebrate vegetables for what they are – nutritious and delicious. I would like to give special thanks to Diana Vowles, my editor, who has been a pleasure to work with (as always) and Bob Bridle who has managed things so efficiently at DK. I would also like to thank my family (and now my children's partners, too) who are used to eating a diverse range of foods at most meals when I am experimenting and testing new creations. They have always been incredibly encouraging and supportive – but are also my greatest critics!

Dorling Kindersley would like to thank: William Reavell for photography; Stuart West for additional recipe photography; Katherine Raj and Nicky Collings for photography art direction; Penny Stephens for food styling; Liz Hippisley for prop styling; Jade Wheaton for the illustrations; Chris Mooney for editorial assistance; Anna Burges-Lumsden, Jan Fullwood, Katy Greenwood, Anne Harnan, and Ann Reynolds for recipe testing; Claire Cross for proofreading; and Susan Bosanko for the index.

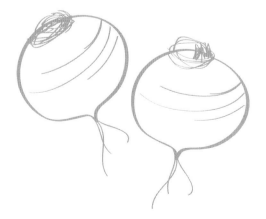